Diversity and the Media

Key Concerns in Media Studies

Series editor: Andrew Crisell

Within the context of today's global, digital environment, *Key Concerns in Media Studies* addresses themes and concepts that are integral to the study of media. Concisely written by leading academics, the books consider the historical development of these themes and the theories that underpin them, and assess their overall significance, using up-to-date examples and case studies throughout. By giving a clear overview of each topic, the series provides an ideal starting point for all students of modern media.

Published

Forthcoming

Diversity and the Media

Monika Metykova

School of Media, Film and Music, University of Sussex, UK

macmillan education   palgrave

First published 2016 by
PALGRAVE

Palgrave Macmillan in the US is a division of St Martin's Press LLC, 175 Fifth Avenue, New York, NY 10010.

Palgrave in the UK is an imprint of Macmillan Publishers Limited, registered in England, company number 785998, of 4 Crinan Street, London, N1 9XW.

Palgrave is a global imprint of the above companies and is represented throughout the world.

Palgrave® and Macmillan® are registered trademarks in the United States, the United Kingdom, Europe and other countries.

ISBN 978-1-137-28599-7   ISBN 978-1-137-28600-0 (eBook)
DOI 10.1007/978-1-137-28600-0

This book is printed on paper suitable for recycling and made from fully managed and sustained forest sources. Logging, pulping and manufacturing processes are expected to conform to the environmental regulations of the country of origin.

A catalogue record for this book is available from the British Library.

A catalog record for this book is available from the Library of Congress.

Contents

Acknowledgements

I would like to thank the *Key Concerns in Media Studies* series editor, Andrew Crisell, for his ongoing support and advice. I cannot exaggerate the role that his encouragement and patience played in the completion of this book project. Special thanks are due to Palgrave Commissioning Editor Lloyd Langman whose enthusiasm about the project did not seem to ebb despite my struggle with deadlines. Staff at Palgrave have been professional, efficient and always ready to help; I would like to thank Jenna Steventon, Nicola Cattini and Tuur Driesser in particular. The manuscript has greatly benefited from Ann Edmondson's meticulous and tireless copyediting. Anonymous reviewers provided constructive suggestions for improving the book draft and I am grateful for those. The usual disclaimers apply though; the responsibility for any errors resides solely with the author.

Introduction

While I was writing this book a number of events unfolded that reflect the significance of diversity and how we – as democratic societies – live and manage it. More than half a million refugees and migrants appeared at European Union (EU) borders in the first eight months of 2015, in addition many thousands lost their lives attempting to cross the Mediterranean Sea from Africa. Haunting images of dead men, women and children circulated in the media and discussions about transnational migration, Europe and the fate of refugees/migrants already in Europe and at its borders evolved over long months. With the growing number of refugees and migrants making their way from the southern edge of the borderless Schengen Europe across the Balkans and on towards the most desired destinations of Germany and Scandinavian countries, the divisions among EU countries became increasingly visible. In September 2015 plans for the relocation of 120,000 refugees were discussed by leaders of EU member states, with the German chancellor Angela Merkel leading the calls for a quota system that would make the distribution of the latest wave of refugees and migrants in Europe fair. The United Kingdom (UK) opted out of an EU refugee sharing system and instead pledged to take in 20,000 Syrian refugees. Some of the 'newly democratic' EU member states – namely the Czech Republic, Hungary, Romania and Slovakia – argued that they were badly prepared for a forced allocation of refugees, and that their incapacity was not only due to the state of their economies but also to their lack of cultural and religious ties with Muslims. They were, however, outvoted and consequently Slovakia and Hungary filed a court challenge against the EU refugee relocation plan.

The argument that Muslim refugees and migrants represent a threat to Europe's Christian identity and values has found its supporters across a variety of countries. While Angela Merkel has insisted that Germany can accept and integrate as many as one million Syrian refugees, Nigel Farage – the leader of UKIP (UK Independence Party), a right-wing populist political party – warned of an African exodus of biblical proportions which should be prevented by restrictive measures. There was, however, one significant exception that Farage was willing to make in his strict opposition to more refugees and migrants entering Britain – Christians should be allowed to come. 'I have said all the way though I particularly feel the plight of Christians because they have nowhere to go in that region, I would happily take some Christian refugees ... Because they have nowhere to go as a direct result of what we've done [that is, the UK's role in removing Muammar Gaddafi in Libya]' (Mason, 2015). The Slovak Prime Minister Robert Fico pointed out that 'refugees have different cultural habits and religion. There is a grave security risk that we must talk about' (Hospodárske noviny, 2015, author's translation). In a comment piece for the German daily newspaper *Frankfurt Allgemeine Zeitung* the Hungarian Prime Minister Viktor Orbán wrote that 'those arriving have been raised in another religion, and represent a radically different culture. Most of them are not Christians, but Muslims. This is an important question, because Europe and European identity is rooted in Christianity' (Mackey, 2015). In the summer of 2015 Hungary embarked on the building of a 175-km long and 4-m high razor fence (which will be turned into a concrete wall at a later stage) along its southern border to stop refugees entering via the so-called Balkan route, and in mid-September it closed its border and introduced a new set of laws that made it a criminal offence – punishable by prison or deportation – to damage the fence. In October Austria and Slovenia announced that they too might have to turn to building fences unless a Europe-wide solution to the refugee crisis was agreed upon.

These events link closely to topics and issues discussed in this book. First of all, Europe has faced a new type of migration – it no longer involves mainly migrants from the (former) colonies to the imperial centres, migrants who had some affinity with the 'host' country. Rather, the refugees and migrants crossing the Mediterranean Sea to the southern borders of Europe are essentially willing to live in any country that is ready to take them. They also connect with other migrants through complex transnational networks and do not necessarily aim to settle in the 'host' country in the long run. Second, as always, the transnational movement of people involves questions of inclusion and exclusion. Farage's preference for Christian refugees indirectly suggests his reservations about Britain accepting Muslims while some East/Central European leaders are much more vocal in their refusal of Muslim refugees. Hence the 2015 refugee crisis raised not only questions about who 'they' (Muslims, refugees, migrants, Syrians) are but equally importantly about who 'we' (Christian, European) are, and about what exactly 'our' way of life is that 'they' supposedly threaten.

The book is thus also concerned with ways that societies develop to manage diversity – through policies and strategies – which have been transforming in European democratic countries since the 1990s when there was a shift from policies of multiculturalism to integration. These policies do not relate only to how many or which refugees are allowed into a country while their asylum claims are processed. They are also linked to how those newly arrived people integrate into their 'host' country and, importantly, they relate to how countries understand or interpret the principles of democratic citizenship. The final observation that I would like to make relates to the role of media in democratic societies. Analyses of the media coverage of the refugee crisis (see for example European Journalism Observatory, 2015) raise important questions about normative ideals linked to the media (that is, how media should perform in democratic societies). In democratic societies the media function as a public sphere in which diverse opinions and views on matters of public importance – and the example of Syrian refugees is one such matter – are given space. Criticisms about the range of opinions and the quality of debate in the media have been wide ranging in relation to the refugee crisis. It is, however, not my aim in this book to make empirically informed judgements about the balance or quality of media representations on any particular issues or in relation to any particular groups; rather, what I offer is the consideration of why and how media policies tackle the broader normative issues and what their limitations are.

Yet, it is not only refugees and migrants – although public discourses tend to focus on them – who are affected by how we manage the co-existence of culturally and ethnically diverse populations. Indigenous minorities and marginalized groups have also fought for democratic citizen rights and cultural rights have been part of this struggle. Media play crucial democratic roles and they are also important for the maintenance of cultures and languages – not having access to channels of communication is disenfranchising. Media systems do not exist in a vacuum, they are the result of government policies and among these are ones intended to promote diversity. There are at least three dimensions of diversity that are relevant for media policy makers, and they are central to the arguments developed in this book – representation of various voices in society; access to a range of communication channels; and a wide range of choice. These different understandings of diversity are reflected in rationales that underpin media regulation, namely effective communication, political diversity and cultural diversity.

It has been widely acknowledged that political as well as analytical discourses are characterized by a lack of clarity when it comes to the concepts of media diversity and media pluralism because the two terms tend to be used interchangeably.

> [M]edia diversity is generally used in a more empirical or tangible meaning, whereas pluralism refers to a more diffuse societal value or an underlying orientation. In the broadest sense, the concept of media diversity refers to the heterogeneity on the level of contents, outlets, ownership or any other aspect of the media deemed relevant.
>
> (Karppinen, 2007, pp. 9–10; cf. Raeijmaekers and Maeseele, 2015)

I use the term 'diversity' throughout the book (apart from references to policy documents using the term 'media pluralism'), both in relation to the broader normative framework of media and democracy and multiculturalism discussed in the first half of the book and in later explorations of diversity at the level of audiences, media workforce and outlets and media contents. This, however, does not mean that the second half of the book is divorced from the normative ideals discussed mainly in Chapters 1, 2 and 3. Indeed, in the 1990s the normative ideals that influence media policy underwent 'a marked pluralistic or anti-essentialist turn ... Instead of a singular notion of the public sphere, national culture or the common good, theorists today prefer stressing the plurality of public spheres, politics of difference, and the complexity of ways in which the media can contribute to democracy' (ibid., p. 11). We should also keep in mind that media policies incorporate contradictory normative ideals; for example, the diversity of representations in the public sphere as well as the maintenance of a national culture into which the various groups in society are integrated (for more on this see Chapter 2 in particular).

In Western European countries public service broadcasting foregrounded the public interest in communication from its inception, while the United States supported competition in a marketplace of ideas that was independent from the intervention of the state. European media systems underwent significant changes when commercial broadcasting was introduced and the regulation of media markets was driven by economic rationales relating to the economic benefits of competitive markets which can involve interventions that intend to remove barriers of entry to markets or tackle concentration. The fact that media are profit-driven industries and important economic players does not come as a surprise. After all, journalists and bloggers report on the box office takings of Hollywood movies on a daily basis, and some of these (although they should not be confused with profits) are staggering. For example, the 2014 Warner Bros re-make of *Godzilla* was heralded as a Box Office King, cashing in over $100 million in its opening week solely on the US market (Box Office Mojo, 2015), while it cost an estimated $160 million to make. Hollywood film studios, however, are not the only content makers that are on investors' radars. The revenues of the Finnish company Rovio – the makers of *Angry Birds* – grew more than 20 fold between 2010 and 2012 (from €6.5 million to €152.2 million) so the company's 2013 annual report (Rovio, 2014) was much anticipated and widely discussed. However, it is important to foreground that competition between media organizations has proved to be insufficient in achieving democratic and social goals because it does not ensure political or cultural diversity, so interventions such as lowering barriers to entry in broadcasting will not ensure optimal outcomes in those areas. Media operate on a dual market, they offer/sell a product to audiences and they sell the audience to advertisers, and we need to bear in mind that they are prone to market failure. This occurs when supply and demand in a market are unequal, as demonstrated by the detrimental impact of ownership concentration on free market competition. Reliance on income from advertising – a crucial funding mechanism for commercial media – reduces the supply of minority programmes because media content will not be made available to an audience that is not sizeable enough nor attractive enough (for example, a low income group) to appeal to advertisers. This is particularly pertinent in the case of ethnic minorities which are often small in size and frequently among low income groups. (In the US, for example, 'the wealth of white households was 13 times the median wealth of black households in 2013'; Kochhar and Fry, 2014.)

Media industries are also on the radar of politicians. They are important businesses with large numbers of employees and – as part of the creative economy – they have been the focus of strategies for job creation and economic growth. Moreover, industries that form part of the creative economy have been identified as providing possible new pathways for economic growth in developing countries (see for example UNESCO and UNDP, 2013). According to UK government data, in 2012 the creative economy accounted for one in twelve jobs or 5.2 per cent of the overall UK economy (Department for Culture, Media and Sport, 2014). Media outputs are bought and sold on international markets and – as US President Barack Obama noted in a 2013 fundraising speech at DreamWorks Studios (the creators of *Shrek* and *Madagascar* among many others) – Hollywood exports are important economically but also 'believe it or not, entertainment is part of our American diplomacy'. The President went on to suggest that Hollywood transmitted US tolerance and diversity to a global audience through its stories:

> They might not know the Gettysburg address, but if they're watching an old movie – *Guess Who's Coming to Dinner*, *The Mary Tyler Moore Show*, or *Will and Grace* and *Modern Family* – they've had a front row seat to our march towards progress. Even if their own nations haven't made that progress yet.
>
> (Carroll, 2013)

Media contents, the ways in which they are produced and the representations that they carry are also of interest to this book although – as already mentioned – my concern here is not predominantly with empirically-based content analyses. It might be presumed that a diverse media workforce will produce diverse contents, but this issue is not so straightforward, as highlighted in a UK-based campaign by the award winning actor Lenny Henry. His campaign for greater ethnic diversity in the British media industry focussed on the public service broadcaster BBC (Conlan, 2014), which indeed earmarked £2.1 million per year for a diversity creative talent fund (BBC, 2014). Although it is without any doubt important to increase the diversity of staff working in media industries (as multiculturalism policies intended to do), focussing solely on public service broadcasters may not be radical enough to achieve change.

It is, however, not only the number of media professionals of minority backgrounds that is of importance here. It has long been documented that women and minority groups face a glass ceiling in the media industries, so it is difficult for them to progress further in the hierarchy than middle management positions. Gender and ethnicity are socially constructed in media organizations – employees may not even be conscious of some entrenched practices that lead to the differential treatment of women or minorities. Also, there may be professional practices and values – for example in the case of journalism those of objectivity and impartiality – that make it difficult to introduce more inclusive ways of representing minorities. Entertainment programmes are not readily associated with democratic roles and policy makers have paid more attention to ensuring political diversity (through interventions in contents, for example) than to representations in entertainment programmes. However, entertainment contents are important for a number of reasons, one of them being the creation of a space in which social values and identities are discussed. This is illustrated by the US sitcom *The Cosby Show* that received critical acclaim and was at the same time criticized for painting an unrealistic picture of an African American family and providing the majority population with an excuse for institutional discrimination.

As already mentioned, democratic governments have been reluctant to introduce policies that could be seen as intervening in media contents – after all freedom of speech is highly valued in these countries – and there have been only a very few signs that this approach may change. One such indication occurred in 2007 when the European Parliament invited the European Commission to propose measures for media pluralism at the European level. In the process the EU commissioned an *Independent Study on Indicators for Media Pluralism in the Member States – Towards a Risk-Based Approach* that will 'develop a monitoring tool for assessing risks for media pluralism in the EU Member States and identifying threats to such pluralism based on a set of indicators, covering pertinent legal, economic and socio-cultural considerations' (Europa, 2015a, p. viii). The inclusion of indicators of cultural diversity has been a major development because the EU normally works with a narrow understanding of media diversity as a competition objective and leaves issues of cultural identity and national culture as constructed and managed by public service broadcasters in the hands of the member states. The pilot project resulted in the so-called Media Pluralism Monitor tool that underwent pilot implementation in 2013 (Europa, 2015b). It is, however, questionable whether it will be implemented by member states. The Media Pluralism Monitor draws attention to the importance of international regulatory bodies when considering how diversity relates to media. Institutions such as the Council of Europe and the United Nations Educational, Scientific and Cultural Organization (UNESCO) have been developing policies related to cultural diversity and, of course, international organizations that deal with trade and competition are also relevant. It is evident that media policy making occurs at the national as well as transnational level and it is embedded in the relevant social and political frameworks. Policy making has evolved historically and reflects shifts in power relations among the various stakeholders. It is not my aim here to provide a comprehensive overview of media policy making within various national and transnational contexts. Instead, I provide examples from countries of the EU (including some of the 'new democracies') and the United States to illustrate the underlying policy rationales and regulatory mechanisms that relate to media diversity in terms of reflecting differences in society, access to channels of communication and finally contents. Whenever possible I attempt to provide at least a brief account of the historical background. As already explained Chapters 1, 2 and 3 focus on the larger norma- tive frameworks, and the subsequent chapters provide more tangible accounts of diversity as reflected in media policy relating to diversity of audiences, media outlets, media producers and contents.

New media technologies have been explored for their potential of empowering marginalized groups in society and also for creating alternative public spheres – spaces in which minority groups can come together and discuss matters that are of importance to them. While the internet has not provided an easily available ready-made solution for dealing with inequalities in democratic societies, there are indica- tions that some online spaces for debate actually provide meaningful alternatives to the national mediated public sphere. Yet, one should be cautious about the extent to which new media technologies increase the diversity of access to channels of communication because some of the most marginalized groups in society still face a digital divide which runs along gender, race and income lines, with the well-off and well- educated making better use of them. In addition, concerns have been raised about new media technologies fragmenting audiences and ena- bling a cosy retreat into echo chambers where one's circles include only those with the same views. The internet has also made the headlines for another reason – the so-called battle for net neutrality. The campaign that aimed to prevent the potential creation of a two-tier internet (a fast lane for the well-off and a slow one for others) highlighted its impor- tance for democratic life and also the fact that, unlike broadcasting, regulation of the internet in the public interest has been largely absent.

The transnational movement of people to which I referred in the opening to the Introduction has been accompanied by the consump- tion of transnational media contents. This may seem to be a recent phenomenon but it dates back to the 19th century and the spread of telegraph which led to the establishment of the first corporations with an international scope and the first international media markets and news industries. The domination of US media products (summarized in phrases such as 'Americanization' or 'Dallasification', referring to the US television series *Dallas*) was opposed particularly vocally in the 1970s and 1980s with discussions about the one-way flow of media products at UNESCO. The concept of cultural imperialism dates back to the late 1960s and was based on the premise that US dominance in media content production led to homogenization and threatened indigenous cultures. Although the concept of cultural imperialism has been largely replaced with that of globalization, scholarly interest in news flows and their unevenness persists. The emergence of alternative news agencies from outside 'the West' (such as Al Jazeera, a Qatari-owned television station which also broadcasts in English) has been linked to the creation of a contra-flow of news. The response of governments to the competitive threat of US media companies has been visible also at the pan-European level with the EU introducing media policies aimed at increasing the competitiveness of the European media industries. The 'Television without Frontiers' Directive of 3 October 1989 created a European common market in television broadcasts and introduced a protective measure – quotas on European works and works produced by independent companies. The EU has also attempted to create a pan-European broadcaster that would promote a European culture and identity, but without much success. Critics of the project point out that it worked with the same assumptions as national broadcasting, and these were inadequate within a transnational context.

Transnational media consumption has also been on the rise particularly since the 1980s when satellite television spread. This is partly due to technological developments that make it easy to access media from a variety of countries, including – in the case of migrants – their countries of origin. Research suggests that migrants enjoy a varied media diet and that transnational contents form only one part of it. In some cases migrants do not find enough contents that are pertinent to them in the mainstream media in their 'host' countries and hence they turn to alternatives, including minority or community media. However, concerns have been raised that this leads to ghettoization or the creation of parallel mediated public spheres and some see this as a sign of migrants' unwillingness to integrate into their new communities. Research into transnational media consumption poses significant issues, which mainly relate to finding conceptualizations that avoid the national frame. New media technologies also enable the creation of major global businesses. For example, three search engines dominate the global market – Google, Yahoo and Microsoft – indeed, in 2015 the European Commission launched an investigation into Google's possible abuse of its dominant position (European Commission, 2015). There are a number of online content providers that represent major business interests, including iTunes, Apple's music streaming service which in 2015 had 800 million accounts globally, and the content streaming service Netflix which reached 75 million users globally.

The writing of this book was also framed by events that put the spotlight on ongoing racial inequalities and (institutional) racism in the United States. The killings and maltreatment of black Americans by law enforcement officers and the subsequent unrest in Chicago, Minneapolis, St Louis and other cities made headlines worldwide. A data journalism project by the UK-based newspaper *The Guardian* worked with statistical data for the first five months of 2015 and found that '29% of those killed by police, or 135 people, were black. Sixty-seven, or 14%, were Hispanic/Latino, and 234, or 50%, were white. ... The figures illustrate how disproportionately black Americans, who make up just 13% of the country's total population according to census data, are killed by police' (Swaine et al., 2015). Moreover, the data analysis showed that unarmed black Americans were twice as likely to be killed by the police as other unarmed people. In June 2015 the pastor and eight parishioners of the Mother Emanuel African American church were killed in a racially motivated attack in Charleston. In his eulogy for Reverend Clementa Pinckney US President Barack Obama spoke about the gap between the discourses of post-race and the actual lived experiences of African Americans in the United States (see Squires, 2014).

Much scholarly work has been devoted to exploring this gap and this book is intended as a contribution to debates about the inequalities that persist in democratic societies. However, the exploration of the (mediated) post-race discourse as such is not central to the arguments discussed in this book. Rather, the central question that the book addresses is the role of media diversity in sustaining a democratic public sphere/s and achieving that within the framework of policy approaches. The book thus builds on approaches and research usually associated with media economics, political economy, political communication and critical media industry studies. Partly due to the focus on policy and the ways in which media policies frame issues of diversity, the book may allude to approaches associated more closely with cultural studies but they are not central to its concerns.

Chapter outline

1 Living and managing diversity

This chapter takes a broader look at the concepts and developments that are crucial for understanding how we – as democratic societies – live diversity and how we manage the co-existence of various ethnic and cultural groups in (super)diverse societies. It provides some statistical data to support the notion that migration has not only increased but its nature has also changed. The chapter traces the shift from policies of multiculturalism to integration that has been ongoing since the 1990s in a number of European countries, and it stresses that managing diversity must be linked to democratic citizenship in order to be inclusive. National culture plays a key role in any discussions about social inclusion, and the chapter argues that the shift away from multiculturalism signals both support for homogenizing understandings of national culture and a faulty understanding of identity as a zero-sum game in which migrants are expected to 'shed' their 'original' identity in order to be included. The chapter concludes with a consideration of the normative framework – how media should operate in order to attain certain social, democratic and other goals. The normative framework, the policies and regulations that guide the operation of media, are decided in the political and judicial arena, and policy responses can be influenced by the politicization of the issues under consideration (migration certainly represents one such issue). The chapter outlines three dimensions of diversity that are relevant for media policy makers – diversity as reflection of differences in society, diversity of access to channels of communication and finally diversity of contents.

2 Media diversity and the public service tradition

Broadcasting was from its early days understood as a public good in Western European democracies and that in the economic sense as well as in a more general philosophical sense as an activity that was to enhance the quality of communal life and contribute to the development of democratic culture. Public service broadcasting is underpinned by a need to provide diverse information to citizens and society at large, and is less concerned with the freedom of communicators. (In this respect it differs significantly from an understanding of the media as a market with competing information.) Jürgen Habermas' concept of the public sphere is relevant for explorations of public service broadcasting in three aspects at least: it stresses that the institutions and practices of mass communication are closely linked to the institutions and practices of democratic societies; a public sphere needs to be independent from the market as well as the state; and it requires a material basis. With the increasing diversification of European societies, public service broadcasting – a quintessentially national cultural institution – faces the challenge of greater inclusivity. The chapter argues that multiculturalism policies – despite their limitations linked to support for particular ethnic groups – aid a more inclusive type of broadcasting. The crisis of public service broadcasting has been linked to marketization (occurring in Europe since the 1980s), and a crisis of legitimacy as well as technological change. The chapter also considers whether the emergence of new media technologies has improved diversity of access to channels of communication, particularly in the light of evidence that the digital divide continues to exist along gender, race and income lines.

3 Media diversity and the marketplace of ideas

This chapter explores a competition-based approach to media and discusses whether such an approach is beneficial for social and cultural goals that are associated with the media. In the United States public service broadcasting did not develop as in Europe; from the beginning it was assumed that competition in the marketplace of ideas was the best approach to ensuring that the truth would emerge. However, concerns about the efficiency of this arrangement were raised early on, and in the 1940s the Fairness Doctrine was introduced to ensure that controversial issues were covered by the media and that contradictory opinions were represented in the marketplace of ideas. The chapter explores the economic characteristics of the media in order to develop the argument that competition-based approaches are not sufficient if we want to ensure that the media fulfil their democratic and social roles. Some of the shortcomings of a competition-based approach arise from the nature of media markets – media operate on a dual market and they are particularly prone to market failure. Interventions in the media market can, for example, aim to secure unhindered competition and deal with barriers to entry to markets but they are not sufficient guarantors of the social and democratic roles of the media. Clearly, media are also important businesses. Economic justifications for regulation play a significant role in this respect and result in benefits for consumers, although arguably these do not necessarily equate to benefits for citizens. The chapter also discusses advertising – a funding model that is crucial for media industries – and demonstrates its shortcomings in respect of the inclusion of minorities.

4 Transnationalization of media and audiences

Media contents travel across national borders and the internationalization of media and their dispersed audiences raises a number of challenges for policy makers as well as scholars. The chapter discusses the development of the transnational media system which is characterized by international media spaces and flows that are no longer the sole preserve of Western-based conglomerates (for example, news organizations like Al Jazeera are seen as providing a contra-flow of news). The chapter considers imbalances in the global news flow and some of the historical developments in this respect. The emergence of a number of transnational media organizations has been driven by profit considerations, although in some cases – such as the pan-European broadcaster – the driving forces have also been linked to cultural identity. Policy makers have responded to the 'Americanization' or 'Dallasification' of European media by introducing measures aimed at increasing the competitiveness of the European media industries and at protecting them from the dominance of US contents. The chapter also considers the relevance of new media technologies within the framework of the transnationalization of media and audiences. The transnational consumption of media is closely linked to migrants' (or minority populations') construction of cultural identity and maintenance of a sense of belonging, but it has been interpreted as being detrimental to their integration into the 'host' society. The study of transnational media consumption poses particular methodological and conceptual challenges, some of which are related to the limitations of a 'national container' viewpoint that sees the national unit as the primary unit of analysis and makes transnational approaches highly problematic.

5 Diversity and media producers

The chapter explores the premise that a diversity of content producers translates seamlessly into a diversity of contents, or in other words, if there are significant numbers of media content producers who belong to/represent marginalized groups, their voices will be heard. This premise is explored in relation to professional journalism and two marginalized groups in particular – women and ethnic minorities. The marginalization of these groups within the journalistic profession and its consequences have been discussed for a number of years (not least in the 1960s in connection with race riots in the US). Women and ethnic minorities are numerically under-represented within the profession and they also face a glass ceiling which limits the positions to which they are promoted. (Women and representatives of ethnic minorities rarely take up positions in the top management of media companies, they often 'get stuck' in middle management.) The chapter argues that there is no simple quantifiable solution because gender and ethnic identities are also constructed within media organizations (organizations are not neutral in their treatment of gender and ethnic differences) and these professional values and practices (independently of who exercises them) can significantly limit the possibilities for improving the representation of women or ethnic minorities. The chapter also considers the 'typecasting' of ethnic minority journalists and the special expectations that they face, not only in representing the groups to which they belong but also in conducting their profession in a way that serves as a bridge between the minority and the majority populations.

6 Diverse societies, diverse contents

The final chapter explores diversity of contents and ways in which democratic societies manage it. Governments of democratic countries have been reluctant to introduce restrictions on contents, after all such measures are associated with totalitarian regimes. However, we find policies that either encourage the production of 'good' contents or suppress 'bad' ones. The chapter considers political diversity measures that relate to news and current affairs and argues that public service broadcasters are more closely regulated and scrutinized in this respect than their commercial counterparts. The focus of the chapter is broadcasting because it has been subjected to statutory regulation more readily than the press, which has traditionally been self-regulated in the United States and Western Europe, although the chapter briefly considers the principles of self-regulation. When exploring entertainment contents and their diversity, the chapter highlights examples of recent television series that are widely understood as examples of complex representations of diversity, including the Canadian series *The Little Mosque on the Prairie* (produced by a public service broadcaster) and the series *Orange is the New Black* (produced by Netflix). Netflix is an example of a commercial online streaming company that has become a competitor in the television content market. Arguably, this increase in the number of market players has contributed to greater diversity of choice and has also prompted traditional cable companies to compete (for example, ABC has commissioned a series about an Asian American family). The final section of the chapter considers the diversity of online contents, restricting the discussion to news and the supposed democratization of journalism which is the result of the greater involvement of 'ordinary' readers, listeners and viewers in decisions over contents and editorial choices.

1 Living and Managing Diversity

After the end of the Second World War European societies have faced challenges linked to migration and to broader issues of how to manage the co-existence of a variety of ethnic/cultural groups. Although the transnational movement of people is by no means a new phenomenon, the more recent waves of migration – which Robins (2007) calls 'migrations of globalization' – differ from the arrival of migrants from former colonies in the post-war years. In the UK the docking of the *Empire Windrush* passenger ship with 492 African Caribbean migrants at Tilbury in June 1948 marked the start of the post-war immigration boom. These passengers travelled from the imperial periphery to its centre and, while we should not dismiss the continued importance of the imperial ties/ imperialism, in more recent migrations, arguably in the 1990s, migrants coming to Europe (for example, from former Yugoslavia) have followed a more random re-location logic and have been dispersed in a number of countries. In addition, Robins (ibid.) argues, another distinctive characteristic of contemporary transnational migration is the networked nature of migrants' economic and social livelihoods that often cross national boundaries. The arrival of 'others' prompts policy responses and in the Introduction I have mentioned some politicians' reactions to the 2015 refugee crisis and particularly verbalizations of the 'Muslim threat'. A series of so-called Islamist terrorist attacks on a global scale – including the 11 September 2001 attacks on the Twin Towers in New York and subsequent terrorist bombings in Madrid on 11 March 2004 and London on 7 July 2005 in London – prompted distinct policy responses.

European governments tend to focus on threats to social cohesion (disintegration of the social fabric, the existence of parallel societies, a lack of integration into mainstream society and similar have all been quoted by politicians) and security (counter-terrorism strategies, deradicalization), and some policy moves also involve a distancing from multiculturalism. In February 2011 David Cameron – the UK Prime Minister – gave a controversial speech at the Munich Security Conference. This was his first speech as Prime Minister on radicalization and the causes of terrorism, and it gave a clear indication of his thoughts on the failures of multiculturalism. He pointed out that 'under the doctrine of state multiculturalism, we have encouraged different cultures to live separate lives, apart from each other and apart from the mainstream' (Cameron, 2011) and he went on to argue that if we are to defeat terrorism, we have to discontinue the failed policies of the past.

> So first, instead of ignoring this extremist ideology, we – as governments and as societies – have got to confront it, in all its forms. And second, instead of encouraging people to live apart, we need a clear sense of shared national identity that is open to everyone.

The Prime Minister also suggested that:

> There are practical things that we can do as well. That includes making sure that immigrants speak the language of their new home and ensuring that people are educated in the elements of a common culture and curriculum.
>
> (ibid.)

Arun Kundnani (2015) argues that associating the cultural roots of home-grown terrorism in the UK with the general trend of young Muslims rethinking their identities leads to the omission of more political factors, including governments' foreign policies. Moreover, this particular focus enables governments to scrutinize a wide range of behaviours as a security threat (so-called indicators of radicalization).

> It also meant that government projects to intervene in the cultural dynamics of Muslim life to try to shore up alternatives to Islamism could be legitimized as part of a counterterrorism strategy ...[and] it implied that multicultural tolerance of these new forms of identity, in which Muslims identify with their coreligionists around the world, was in itself a national security risk.
>
> (Kundnani, 2015, p. 39)

Cameron's speech highlights issues that are of central concern to this chapter and to the whole book. What does a shared national culture involve? How open is it to cultural difference? And is it democratic? Why is media policy important in this respect? These are some questions that this chapter addresses.

Multiculturalism policies came to the forefront in democratic societies in the 1960s, and they were intended to address ethnic/cultural
diversity in more inclusionary ways than the previously favoured
assimilationist policies. In some countries (Canada and Australia)
multiculturalism has been embraced at the highest levels of government as official policy. '[S]ince the mid-1990s we have, however, seen
a backlash and retreat from multiculturalism, and a reassertion of ideas
of nation building, common values and identity, and unitary citizenship – even a call for the "return of assimilation"' (Kymlicka, 2012,
p. 2). Kymlicka also points out that this retreat does not only characterize populist right-wing political parties in Europe but also centre-left
political movements that originally championed multiculturalism but
moved away because of its failure to address the underlying sources of
the social, political and economic exclusion of minorities and because
its policies may have (unintentionally) contributed to that social exclusion (ibid.). This chapter discusses developments in the way diversity
is understood and managed in contemporary democratic societies, and
how these impact on the ways in which media are expected to operate.
The final section of the chapter is concerned with normative aspects –
how media should operate to achieve particular goals linked to the
democratic co-existence of various groups within society – rather than
with assessing the actual operation of media.

Living multi-culture, living (super)diversity

The fact that we live in culturally diverse societies is reflected in our
everyday lived experience, 'European culture and society have become
more and more complex and diverse. Diversity and complexity are
now a de facto presence in European social and cultural life, not the
aspiration or fantasy of idealistic cosmopolitan intellectuals' (Robins,
2007, p. 160). Statistical data can give us a sense of the changing demographic make-up of societies: 'Between 1993 and 2014 the foreign-born
population in the UK more than doubled from 3.8 million to around
8.3 million. During the same period, the number of foreign citizens
increased from nearly 2 million to more than 5 million' (Rienzo and
Vargas-Silva, 2015, p. 2). The numbers of people moving into and
within the European Union are also telling: 'In 2012, the population of
the EU included 34.3 million foreign citizens, representing 6.8% of the
total population. ... More than one third (13.6 million) of these people
were citizens of another EU Member State' (Eurostat, 2015). According

to EU data, Germany is among the countries with the highest numbers
of immigrants and the most recent statistics available from the German
Federal Statistical Office at the time of writing (October 2015) state
that:

> 1,226,000 people immigrated to Germany in 2013. This was an
> increase of 146,000, or 13%, from 2012. Such a high level of immi-
> gration was last recorded in 1993 [it involved refugees escaping
> the wars in Yugoslavia]. A total of 789,000 people departed from
> Germany in 2013, 77,000 (+11%) more than in the previous year.
> Balancing arrivals against departures results in a net immigration
> of 437,000 people in 2013 – also the highest figure since 1993.
>
> (DESTATIS, 2015)

These trends, of course, do not apply only to Europe, as suggested
by a random selection of data from reports on social and demographic
trends in the United States published by the Pew Research Center.

> The number of immigrants in the U.S. doubled from 23 million
> people in 1990 to 46 million in 2013. During this time, no other
> country has come close to the number of foreign-born people
> living within its borders. For example, second-ranked Russia had
> about 11 million immigrants in both 1990 and 2013 (many of
> whom had moved within the former USSR prior to 1990).
>
> (Connor et al., 2013)

> A record 3.8 million black immigrants live in the United States
> today, more than four times the number in 1980, according to a
> Pew Research Center analysis of U.S. Census Bureau data. Black
> immigrants now account for 8.7% of the nation's black popula-
> tion, nearly triple their share in 1980.
>
> (Anderson, 2015)

> Between 2000 and 2010, the number of white and black biracial
> Americans more than doubled, while the population of adults with
> a white and Asian background increased by 87% ... The share of
> multiracial babies has risen from 1% in 1970 to 10% in 2013.
>
> (Pew Research Center, 2015, p. 6)

Cities have also been noted for their degree of ethnic and cultural
diversity. London has long been considered one of the major cosmopolitan cities in the world. According to 2014 data 36.6% of London's

inhabitants were born abroad (compared to the national average of 13%) and 2011 data reveal that the largest migrant population by country of birth is Indian (3.2% of London's overall population), followed by Polish (1.9%) and Irish (1.6%). When considering ethnicity, data from 2013 show that 41.8% of London's population belongs to Black, Asian and minority ethnic groups, compared to 14.6% nationally (Greater London Authority, 2015). And finally when it comes to languages: 'A language other than English is the main language of about 1.7 million residents of London (22% of the London population). ... From those with a main language other than English, close to 9% selected Polish as their main language, followed by Bengali (7%) and Gujarati (6%)' (Krausova and Vargas-Silva, 2013). In 2008, the first year that the Annual School Census explored the distribution of languages spoken in London state schools, it found 118 different languages (Greater London Authority, 2015a) while the Greater London Authority's '20 Facts about London's Culture' lists the following fact: 'There are more than 300 languages spoken in London, more than in any other city in the world' (Mayor of London, 2015).

Steven Vertovec argues that in the case of Great Britain it is not only the increased migrations from a larger variety of places that matter, he uses the term 'super-diversity' to highlight the fact that 'significant new conjunctions and interactions of variables have arisen through patterns of immigration to the UK over the past decade; their outcomes surpassed the ways – in public discourse, policy debates and academic literature – we usually understand diversity in Britain'. He then calls on social scientists and policy makers 'to take more sufficient account of the conjunction of ethnicity with a range of other variables when considering the nature of various "communities", their composition, trajectories, interactions and public service needs' (2007, p. 1025). In other words, as our societies get more diverse, the diversity that characterizes them is also more complex and in order to understand and manage this complex diversity in inclusionary ways, we need to develop new scholarly and policy approaches. There is – understandably – a prevalent agreement among political elites also that inclusion is desirable. However, the ways in which it can (and should be) achieved are more divisive. Although there are developments that are shared across democratic societies, there are also significant differences and there is not enough space in this chapter to discuss those in detail. I only pay attention to one example here, that of Germany, where changes in immigration policy since the early 2000s signalled a significant shift in the country's national narrative. This shift was also visible during the summer of 2015 in relation to the re-location of Syrian refugees, with Chancellor Angela Merkel pledging to take in as many as a million of them.

Germany has been viewed as a country with immigration policies focussed on exclusion (see for example Brubaker, 1992). In Helen Williams' discussion of the historical background to the national debate about whether or not Germany is a country of immigration, she points out that 'direct proclamations that Germany was not a country of immigration began to appear frequently under the chancellorship of Helmut Schmidt' and goes on to argue that 'by the early 1980s, much of the immigrant population had already been present for some time, but both Germany and its guestworkers laboured under the impression that their immigration was only temporary' (2014, p. 57).

It took until the early 2000s for a shift in Germany's nationality and immigration policies to occur. The Nationality Act introduced in 2000 reduced:

> the residence requirement for naturalization from 15 to eight years. Ius soli was broadened, allowing children of foreigners with permanent settlement status to be born with German citizenship. Although still officially against dual nationality, Germany's stance was relaxed to allow EU citizens to hold dual nationality in cases of reciprocity and to recognize a greater number of circumstances in which giving up the previous nationality would cause the applicant undue hardship. ... Children born in Germany were given German nationality if born to resident foreigners who would themselves qualify for naturalization because of status and length of residence. If these children simultaneously inherited the foreign nationality of one of their parents through descent-based modes, they were only to be allowed to continue as dual nationals until adulthood.
>
> (ibid., p. 59)

The Nationality Act was followed by the Immigration Act that came into force in 2005 (for details see Federal Foreign Office, 2015), and this shift in German self-understanding leads Williams to conclude that 'on the whole, German elite discourse appears to be growing more liberal and more stable, and the country appears to be establishing a new discursive norm that is more inclusive and exhibits more elements of reciprocal integration' (ibid., p. 73).

From assimilation to multiculturalism

In an often quoted passage Stuart Hall suggests that:

> It might be useful to draw a distinction here between 'multi-cultural' and 'multiculturalism'. Here multi-cultural is used adjectivally. It describes the social characteristics and problems of governance posed by any society in which different cultural communities live together and attempt to build a common life while retaining something of their 'original' identity. By contrast 'multiculturalism' is substantive. It references the strategies and policies adopted to govern or manage the problem of diversity or multiplicity which multi-cultural societies throw up.
>
> (Hall, 2000, p. 209)

In a similar way, Charles Husband stresses that accounts of multiculturalism do not merely provide 'a descriptive account of ethnic diversity, it [multiculturalism] is always also a political philosophy of how these diverse ethnic identities are supposed to coexist' (2000, p. 200). Scholarship on multiculturalism alerts us to the wider historical and political contexts within which it developed (see for example Pitcher, 2009 and Gilroy, 2002 on the British case; Kymlicka, 2003 and Tierney, 2007 on Canada). Kymlicka situates multiculturalism within the post-Second World War 'human rights revolution' linked to three waves of political movements that favoured the new ideology of equality of people and races:

> 1) the struggle for decolonization, concentrated in the period 1948 to 1965; 2) the struggle against racial segregation and discrimination, initiated and exemplified by the African-American civil rights movement from 1955 to 1965; and 3) the struggle for multiculturalism and minority rights, which emerged in the late 1960s.
>
> (2012, p. 6)

These movements contributed to 'democratic citizenization' by turning hierarchical relationships into those of democratic citizenship. This, however, does not mean that no group-differentiated ethnopolitical claims have been involved but that, rather than suppressing them, they should be framed within the language of human rights, civil liberties and democratic accountability. And this is what multiculturalist movements have aimed to do (ibid., see also Kymlicka, 1995). In the 1960s the governing elites in the UK

> looked anxiously across the Atlantic at the urban uprisings occur-
> ring in the US and hoped they could avoid similar problems by
> passing immigration laws to close the colonial 'open door' to
> those who were not white at the same time that they implemented
> antidiscrimination measures to integrate the new communities of
> colour. In the event, official efforts to end racial discrimination
> proved largely symbolic, while the new immigration laws wors-
> ened matters by reinforcing the perception that people of colour
> were not really part of Britain, conveniently erasing the colonial
> history that had brought them there. A. Sivanandan, a Sri Lankan
> writer who had settled in London in 1958, refused this false sepa-
> ration of immigration from imperialism by inventing the slogan:
> 'We are here because you were there'.
>
> (Kundnani, 2015, p. 32)

In the UK the term 'multiculturalism' emerged in the 1970s and the initial policy focus was on schooling.

> Multiculturalism meant the extension of the school, both in terms
> of curriculum and as an institution, to include features such as
> 'mother-tongue' teaching, black history, Asian dress and – impor-
> tantly – non-Christian religions and holidays, religious dietary
> requirements and so on. It was criticized by socialists and anti-
> racists as not focusing on the real social divisions and causes of
> inequality, and caricatured as a preoccupation with 'saris, steel
> bands and samosas'. ... One consequence was a perhaps unneces-
> sary and prolonged division between anti-racists and multicultur-
> alists; another was that religious issues were marginalized, even by
> advocates of multicultural education.
>
> (Modood and Ahmad, 2007, p. 188)

By the 1990s, however, there was a growing recognition that the dimensions of citizenship identified classically by T.H. Marshall (1950) – civic, political and social – might be extended to include cultural entitle-ments. 'What began to be recognized was the value of cultural empower-ment in the citizen body as a whole, involving the capacity on the part of all citizens to participate fully and creatively in national cultural life – accepted as diverse and complex cultural life' (Robins 2007, p. 161).

Although public discourses of the 2000s may give the impression that multiculturalism was a model based on the 3Ss – 'saris, steel bands and samosas' (see also Alibhai-Brown, 2000) – as Kymlicka and Hall both explain, the everyday manifestations of the 'mixing' of cultures are actually different from multiculturalism policies and strategies that have promoted minority cultural rights as much as political and economic equality.

In addition, importantly, policies developed within a multiculturalism framework have involved not only immigrant groups (on whom current political and public discourses tend to focus) but also historic minorities and indigenous peoples that suffered exclusion. As already mentioned multiculturalism policies and strategies replaced earlier assimilationist policies that were based – as their name suggests – on the premise that

> immigrants assimilate when they become similar to natives ... The term can be used empirically, to describe what immigrants actually do – but it can also be used normatively, to indicate what many natives *expect* immigrants to do (with such expectations typically rooted in ethnocentrism [the belief or presumption that the destination country's culture is superior to that of the immigrant's country of origin] or even outright prejudice).
>
> (Bartram et al., 2014, pp. 15 and 16, original emphasis)

Wimmer criticizes the classic assimilation paradigm in migration studies for assuming that

> the boundaries of culture, category/identity, and community coincide in an unproblematic way. The units of analysis are communities of immigrants from a particular country of origin who make their way into the social mainstream. At the end of the process, the communities are dissolved through intermarriage and spatial dispersion, minority cultures are diluted through processes of acculturation, and ethnic identities become ever thinner until all that remains is what Herbert Gans has famously called 'symbolic ethnicity'.
>
> (Wimmer, 2007, p. 4)

In his influential study Gans hypothesized that 'in this [3rd] generation, people are less and less interested in their ethnic cultures and organizations – both sacred and secular – and are instead more concerned with maintaining their ethnic identity, with the feeling of being Jewish, or Italian, or Polish, and with finding ways of feeling and expressing that identity in suitable ways' (1979, p. 7). He went on to argue that 'in other words, as the functions of ethnic cultures and groups diminish and identity becomes the primary way of being ethnic, ethnicity takes on an expressive rather than instrumental function in people's lives, becoming more of a leisure-time activity and losing its relevance, say, to earning a living or regulating family life' (ibid., p. 9).

Even this brief account should make it clear that multiculturalism and assimilationism are based on radically different expectations of what the co-existence of diverse cultural and ethnic groups in a democratic society should be like. However, both multiculturalism and assimilationism work with a group-based approach which has its limitations. For example, Wimmer (2007) and Robins (2007) find the focus on clearly demarcated groups within the national container highly problematic. In seeking better alternatives Wimmer suggests a focus on boundary making while Robins proposes a transnational (as opposed to national) perspective.

From multiculturalism to integration or back to (new) assimilation?

As already suggested, from the mid-1990s we can detect a shift away from multiculturalism to integration policies. This, however, does not mean that civic integration policies have completely replaced multiculturalism ones. Titley (2014) refers to Derek McGhee's observation that in the UK multiculturalism as a term has been driven underground at the level of national debate but the logic of multiculturalism actually continues to inform policy. Similarly, Kymlicka (2012) demonstrates that despite the retreat from multiculturalism, multiculturalism policies have actually persisted.

> [In migration studies] the core meaning of integration has to do with increasing social membership for migrants in the destination country. At least in an analytical sense, one can distinguish between integration and assimilation by noting that integration of immigrants can occur without their becoming highly similar to natives (assimilation), particularly in cultural terms.
>
> (Bartram et al., 2014, p. 84)

Because integration involves social membership, it has been studied in relation to a range of indicators including political affiliation, education, cultural capital and so on. Integration has become a major part not only of academic research in general but specifically of policy research, with research centres and policy think tanks devoted to the study of the integration of immigrants. For example, the Stanford University's Immigration and Integration Policy Lab home page states that:

> The Lab's goal is to create a deeper and balanced understanding of immigrant integration to help inform and advance policy. Ultimately, improving integration can reduce native backlash against immigrants, reduce social tension, increase national security and unleash the full economic potential of immigrants. We are dedicated to advancing immigration policy through quality research in order to improve lives.
>
> (Stanford University, 2015)

Kymlicka argues that civic integration and multiculturalism are not necessarily at odds with each other, although he identifies two potential sources of conflict between them. The first is a shift from rights to duties, making integration a duty and linking it, for example, to access to social policy provisions goes against the principles of multiculturalism.

> There has been a shift toward the idea that citizens have to fulfil certain duties before they can claim certain rights. ... If indeed such policies are imposed on all citizens, then they are not inherently anti-immigrant or antidiversity (although some of us are likely to view them as an erosion of basic liberal or social-democratic values). But the shift from rights to duties raises a danger that those groups deemed 'unworthy' of being treated as rights-bearing individuals – in particular, non-white, non-Christian immigrants – will be targeted. Insofar as perceptions of the unworthiness of immigrants underpin coercive integration policies, then a coercive integration strategy negates multicultural affirmation of diversity.
>
> (2012, p. 17; see also Lentin and Titley, 2011,
> particularly Chapter 5 – Good and bad diversity:
> The shape of neoliberal racisms)

The second source of conflict between multiculturalism and integration 'concerns the definition of the national culture that immigrants are integrated into (coercively or voluntarily), and how open it is to the visible maintenance and expression of difference' (ibid., p. 17). If national identity is understood as a zero-sum game, immigrants are expected to shed their 'old' identity (or at least subordinate it and possibly hide it for public purposes), which is clearly contradictory to multiculturalism. Indeed, the shift towards a reassertion of a unitary national identity and culture – evident in David Cameron's speech, for example – also signals a shift to a homogenizing discourse that captures

> an inherent resistance to those who do not have things in common, who do not belong – 'them', meaning both outsiders and diverse populations within. Those within are marginalized, or minoritized, in order not to compromise the 'clarity' of the imagined community. And with respect to the others outside, the national community seeks to differentiate itself, to maintain its fundamental discreteness, protecting its borders and asserting its sovereignty; to belong to the community is to be contained within a bounded culture. Imagined in this sense, the community is always fated to anxiety. The coherence and integrity of what is held in common must always be conserved and sustained against diversity and complexity, which come to be represented as forces of disintegration and potential dissolution.
>
> (Robins, 2007, p. 151)

In 2006 Ambalavaner Sivanandan, writer and Director Emeritus of the Institute of Race Relations, a London-based independent educational charity, remarked that 'to use "integration" and "assimilation" as synonyms ... is not just to misuse language and confuse concepts, but to dissimulate practice. Integration is what they say, assimilation is what they do' (Sivanandan, 2006). There has been a re-visiting of assimilation in the scholarly community and some academic accounts of the retreat from multiculturalism suggest that a return to assimilation is not as problematic as it may first appear. For example, Rogers Brubaker (2001) argues that 'when used *intransitively* in the general, abstract sense of becoming similar – becoming similar *in certain respects*, that obviously have to be specified – assimilation does *not* seem to be morally objectionable, analytically useless, or empirically wrong as a conceptual instrument for studying populations of immigrant origin' (p. 534, original emphasis).

Wimmer, however, argues that 'new' versions of assimilation theory revised some of the assumptions of the 'old' one but they still focus on the same end – assimilation into the mainstream.

Newer versions of assimilation theory foresee different possible end results of the process, including persistent non-assimilation of immigrant communities. ... Two new outcomes are added to the tableau. First, ethnic communities/identities/cultures may persist over time and allow individuals to achieve upward social mobility without having to develop social ties with mainstreamers, without having to acculturate to mainstream culture, and without necessarily identifying with the national majority. Besides this ethnic enclave mode of immigrant incorporation, there is a 'downward assimilation' path where immigrants develop social ties with, identify with, and acculturate to the black segment of American society, rather than the 'white mainstream'.

(2007, p. 4)

We find a number of empirical studies that aim to explore whether assimilation also found its place in public discourses, particularly those promoted by policy makers and opinion leaders. For example, Awad and Roth (2011) conclude that in the Netherlands in public discourse:

One's cultural identity – if different from the dominant Dutch identity – is treated as an impediment to civic participation ... in that sense, the current discourse is assimilationist: it compels cultural minorities to adapt to a dominant model of Dutchness, under the assumption that a well-functioning democracy requires protecting a fixed national identity.

(pp. 404–5)

As, for example, Kymlicka argues this is clearly in contrast with multiculturalism policies. Awad and Roth contend that assimilation is inherently undemocratic because it 'always implies coming into the game after it has already begun, after the rules and standards have already been set, and having to prove oneself according to those standards' (Young as quoted in Awad and Roth, 2011, p. 405).

The turn to integration further involves a deliberately structured gap between the discursive and the material: *integration politics* involves extensive, formal and symbolic demands for loyalty and elective homogeneity in public space, while *integration regimes* organize presence and access to socio-economic rights through stratified systems of entry, status, residence and legitimacy.

(Titley, 2014, p. 251, original emphasis)

Lentin and Titley argue that the rejection of multiculturalism is not necessarily a wholesale rejection of multiculturalism policies and strategies.

[Rather,] the contemporary politics of cultural correction must be resituated in an understanding of racism in a post-racial era. Undoing the relativist experiment and asserting the new realism of cultural incompatibility and hierarchy is based on an assumption that when 'race' and racism were exclusively linked to skin colour and phenotype, they were historical aberrations. ... It is the historical reduction of anti-racist politics to questions of cultural recognition and the excision of 'race' as a political category in favour of culture, that makes possible the claim from various political positions that we are post-race.

(2012, p. 126)

In the UK migrant integration became highly politicized in the early 2000s 'following a national focusing event ("milltown riots" in 2001) and international focusing events (9/11). This led to a policy reframing where, rather than celebrating diversity, policy initiatives began to emphasize activities and values shared in common under the heading of "community cohesion"' (Scholten and Verbeek, 2015, p. 194). Worley argues that the 'language of community' in the community cohesion rhetoric led to a deracialization (2005, p. 491). The de-ethnicization of diversity and its implications have been noted by other scholars as well.

If actors such as the state have learned to speak the language of diversity and anti-racism, becoming fluent in a progressive idiom of race while simultaneously maintaining and consolidating racist practices, then anti-racism is confronted with the crucial problem of maintaining hold on a critical discourse which has to all intents and purposes fallen into the hands of its adversaries.

(Pitcher, 2009, p. 14)

The United States President Barack Obama became more vocal about the limits of the post-race discourse in his eulogy for Reverend Clementa Pinckney, the pastor of the Mother Emanuel African American church who was shot dead together with eight of his parishioners in June 2015, suggesting that:

Maybe we now realize the way racial bias can infect us even when we don't realize it, so that we're guarding against not just racial slurs, but we're also guarding against the subtle impulse to call Johnny back for a job interview but not Jamal. So that we search our hearts when we consider laws to make it harder for some of our fellow citizens to vote.

(White House, 2015)

Media, diversity, policy

Kymlicka stresses that it is important to bear in mind that multiculturalism is first and foremost characterized by the aim of building new models of democratic citizenship to replace earlier undemocratic relationships of exclusion and hierarchy. This underlying principle also has a bearing on media – an issue that is discussed in detail in Chapter 2 in relation to public service broadcasting, a national institution that is mandated to cater for the needs of minority groups. The question of the inclusion/exclusion of cultural groups in the mediated public sphere is highly pertinent, not only because of the importance of the mediated public sphere for democracy (as discussed in Chapter 2) but also for the construction of cultural identities and indeed national culture. Moreover, 'public discursive arenas are among the most important and underrecognized sites in which social identities are constructed, deconstructed, and reconstructed' (Fraser, 1993, p. 140). Mediated spaces have been sites of struggle and negotiation and the emergence of multicultural television programming, for example, should not be understood as a straightforward process.

> The introduction of multicultural television programming, for instance, was described by William Whitelaw, then the Home Secretary, in the following terms: If you are Home Secretary in any government, you are going to take the view that there are a lot of minority interests in this country, [for example] different races. If they don't get some outlet for their activities you are going to run yourself into much more trouble.
>
> (Kundnani, 2015, p. 33)

Multiculturalism has also impacted on the ways in which media are regulated and what is expected of them, 'although not without its own politics of limitation and ghettoization, this [UK] version of state multiculturalism should be noted for being written into media policy and commissioning structures and for being grounded in a particular (albeit soft) version of anti-racism' (Malik, 2013, p. 230). Chapter 2 explores in more detail the shift from multiculturalism to diversity policies and how these impacted on public service broadcasters in particular. However, the final section of this chapter considers the wider issue of the place of diversity in media policy, defined in a broad sense. (For a detailed discussion on the boundaries of media policy in relation to information policy in particular, see Braman, 2004.)

It is important to consider multiculturalism/diversity within a media policy framework because, to borrow Des Freedman's concise opening sentences to his book, *The Politics of Media Policy*:

> Media systems do not emerge spontaneously from the logic of communication technologies, or from the business plans of media corporations, or from the imaginations of creative individuals. ... [M]edia systems are instead purposefully created, their characters shaped by competing political interests that seek to inscribe their own values and objectives on the possibilities facilitated by a complex combination of technological, economic and social factors.
>
> (2008, p. 1)

Normative issues – how the media should operate if certain goals (social values among them) are to be attained – concerning the media in general have long been decided in the political and judicial arenas. As a result a wide range of principles concerning the role of media is reflected in policy documents.

> Policies in general refer to conscious (public) projects for achieving some goal, together with the proposed means and time schedule for achieving them. The specific content of government policies reflects the deal made in the particular time and place and the balance of power and advantage between government and industry.
>
> (van Cuilenburg and McQuail, 2003, p. 182)

In Ellen Goodman's definition media policy 'consists of regulatory interventions specifically designed to promote communicative opportunities' (2007, p. 1211). It is also important to keep in mind that the policy making process involves a range of actors who:

> make claims within a political system on behalf of goals (favoured end-states) which are said, in the light of certain fundamental, or commonly held, values to be of general benefit to the whole society, community or public, over and above individual wants, satisfactions or utilities. These claims are specified in terms of preferences about a communication system or its performances which correspond to the advocated end-state.
>
> (McQuail, 1992a, p. 27)

Although policy making may appear to be a neutral, largely administrative and technical process, actually,

> policy practice is a decisive arena in which different political preferences are celebrated, contested or compromised. This is far from the mechanical or administrative picture that is often painted, whereby faceless civil servants draft legislation on the advice of 'experts' and 'scientists', in the interests of a 'public' and at the behest of a 'responsible' government.
>
> (Freedman, 2008, p. 3)

Indeed, there have been two opposing understandings of the relationship between scientific research and policy.

> The rational model ... that has provided the basis for modern government involved a strongly institutionalized dialogue structure that enabled scientific experts to have a relatively strong primacy in policy-making. In terms of research–policy relations, this has often been described in terms of a technocratic model that enabled science to 'speak truth to power'. ... Technocracy involves formal and direct forms of policy involvement by scientific experts and is usually associated with a culture of depoliticization.
>
> (Scholten and Verbeek, 2015, p. 189)

Alternatively, '[i]n politicized settings, research and expertise are much less likely to be used as an authoritative source of policy-making, as this could be interpreted as a threat to political primacy. When expertise itself becomes increasingly politicized, research–policy relations are more likely to vary over time with shifts in political power' (ibid., p.189).

As already suggested, multiculturalism – as a way of managing multi-culture – had an impact on the creation of tools that would enable the greater inclusion of minorities. I return to this point in more detail in Chapter 2. Within the framework of media policy, multiculturalism is closely linked to pluralism. Within the media policy context – as explained in the Introduction – pluralism is understood as a societal value that is one of the constitutive tenets of liberal democracy. As Raeijmaekers and Maeseele (2015) argue, pluralism 'has to be located on the ontological dimension of the social: it regards ideological differences, such as discursive practices and strategies in the (re)production of identities and concerns (differences *about* society)' (p. 1051, original emphasis). Karppinen points out that pluralism appears to be a value that is readily embraced and referred to, yet its meaning is somewhat obscure. We should also keep in mind that in media policy,

> pluralism – as a concept – clearly alludes to objectivity and neutral-ity that seem to transcend the dilemmas inherent in terms such as quality or social responsibility in assessing media performance. While this makes it more compatible with both the needs of technocratic expert assessment and the broader ideology of anti-paternalism and multiculturalism, it can also be argued that this inclusiveness and indeterminacy serves to mask political conflicts and antagonisms in media policy and is thereby often obscuring the properly political or normative aspects of evaluating media performance and setting policy objectives.
>
> (2007, p. 12)

Diversity has played a significant role in the shaping of media policy – and that at least in two ways. It can serve, on the one hand, as an underpinning for regulatory interventions (for example, when diversity as a policy objective is related to political and social/cultural values) and, on the other, as an indicator in assessments of performance. Pub-lic service broadcasters provide regular reports on their performance and these often include analyses of the diversity of contents produced by them. I will offer concrete examples of such interventions through-out the book but it is important to discuss some of the more general issues involved here. We should keep in mind that diversity is not an end in itself but a means of enabling media to play their roles in rela-tion to important democratic values (equality, social inclusion and so on). We can distinguish at least three dimensions of diversity that are relevant to media policy makers because media can contribute to diversity 'by *reflecting* differences in society; by giving *access* to different points of view and by offering a wide range of *choice*' (McQuail, 1992a, p. 144, original emphasis). Diversity as reflection relates mainly to the representation of 'prevailing differences of culture, opinion and social conditions of the population as a whole' (ibid.), which is most closely related to media contents, although arguably it can also be linked to the structure of the media system. Diversity as access refers to access to channels (made available by media) for various voices (that is, groups and interests which the society comprises), and McQuail stresses that the most essential preconditions for access are 'freedom to speak out; effective opportunity to speak (the existence of a sufficient number of independent and different channels); autonomy, or adequate self-control over media access opportunities' (ibid., p. 145). The third dimension of diversity refers to the choice of products and services available. Athough McQuail considers further conceptualizations and categorizations of diversity (see Chapter 11 in particular), these three dimensions will be recurring themes throughout the book.

Feintuck and Varney link the above mentioned dimensions of diversity to two rationales underlying media regulation: effective communication and diversity (political and cultural). Effective communication is linked to the freedom of speech ideal:

In the modern context, in which meaningful freedom of communication depends heavily upon access to mass media, effective communication has come to rely increasingly upon media. Were all communication channelled or controlled exclusively through state controlled media this would run counter to the liberal-democratic ideal of freedom of communication. However, the same argument would seem to apply were the media to be effectively under the control of one or a handful of media owners, a situation of private monopoly or oligopoly.

(2006, p. 59)

Van Cuilenburg argues that:

A high degree of accessibility of communications – the degree to which it is possible to take a share in society's communication resources – indicates a high degree of social inclusion of all groups and people in society, whereas limited access to society's communications resources usually goes with communicative inequality and social exclusion of many groups and individuals.

(1999, p. 185)

Although diversity as a regulatory rationale is linked to effective communication, political and cultural diversity can be presented as separate rationales. 'Political debate, supposedly the lifeblood of democracy, appears to need a free flow of ideas via which informed participation can take place' (Feintuck and Varney, 2006, p. 59). In terms of cultural diversity:

There would be wide-ranging agreement that the provision of programming relevant to varying groups based on race, gender, age, sexual orientation or other social variants, is a positive development. 'Alternative' or non-mainstream television is thought to serve a particular function in reducing social exclusion and this in effect provides the justification for the insertion of specific requirements to this effect in Channel 4's licence [Channel 4 is a UK broadcaster which was granted a licence in 1982].

(ibid., p. 61)

Media play a key role in maintaining culture (on the relationship between national culture and public service broadcasting see Chapter 2), and some countries (for example, France) have been noted for protectionist cultural and language policies, particularly as a reaction to the dominance of US media products (see also Chapter 4). However, media regulation has also been closely watched by members of minority ethnic groups for whom access to media may equate to the survival of their culture and language. Media are among areas in which minority languages need protection (see de Varennes, 1996; on indigenous European minority language television campaigns, see Hourigan, 2001). Of course, through its policies the state unavoidably promotes some cultures over others because state and ethnicity are not strictly separated (Kymlicka 1995).

The rationales outlined above provide some answers to why media are regulated and the regulatory provisions manifest themselves in different ways in different media systems. The scope of this chapter does not allow a discussion of the history of media regulation or an extensive overview of its basic principles. There is a range of literature available on these, including Mansell and Raboy (2011) on the global context, Lunt and Livingstone (2012) on the UK, Freedman (2008) on the UK and the US, Sarikakis (2007) on the EU. Throughout the book I offer accounts of how media are regulated and that specifically in relation to diversity. The US media regulatory framework focusses on competition as a way of achieving policy goals, including ones related to diversity and is in this respect very distinct from European media systems and policies. The Federal Communications Commission (FCC) – the US communications regulator – 'defined diversity as five distinctive yet interrelated concepts, namely, viewpoint, program, outlet, source, and minority and women ownership diversity' (McCann, 2013, p. 4). The first two concepts are linked to diversity of content while the latter three refer to ownership diversity. 'Insisting on the presumed link between ownership diversity and content diversity, the FCC has attempted to create viewpoint and program diversity through outlet, source, and workforce diversity. This explains that the FCC regulatory concepts center primarily on competition of ownership to achieve diversity goals' (ibid.).

> [In contrast, the] public service tradition in Western Europe has served to insulate the media partially from what are perceived as the worst excesses of market forces. Certainly, European (and especially British) television output as a whole has historically been generally compared favourably, in terms of diversity and quality, with the US equivalent which has developed in the absence of a strong PSB [public service broadcasting] tradition.
>
> (Feintuck and Varney, 2006, p. 40)

The public service tradition, its underlying principles and the changes that it faces in the context of marketization and the emergence of new media technologies are discussed in the next chapter.

Other areas of policy that are developed at national as well as international level have an effect on how diversity impacts on media policy. Such legislation can include equality and diversity laws, in the case of European Union countries EU-wide competition law will have an influence and so will regulatory frameworks developed within the Council of Europe (such as the Declaration on Cultural Diversity) or the United Nations (for example, UNESCO Convention on Cultural Diversity). Policies on minority languages and their maintenance also inter-relate with diversity issues. For example, the European Charter for Regional or Minority Languages developed within the Council of Europe includes a whole article devoted to the role of the media in the maintenance of minority languages and specifies the participation of users of minority and regional languages in bodies set up by law that are responsible for guaranteeing the freedom and pluralism of the media (see Article 11 in Council of Europe, 1992). This book discusses examples of media policies from a variety of national contexts (mainly European ones but also the United States because its regulatory frameworks provide an interesting comparative perspective). Its scope does not include an in-depth account of transnational policy making, yet it is important to note the transnational dimension of cultural diversity policies.

> Diversity policies are now being pulled into both an international and a transnational frame of reference. First, we have seen a move – largely as a consequence of the interventionist role of transnational European institutions, notably the European Commission and the Council of Europe – toward a Europe-wide harmonization of national approaches and strategies for cultural diversity. Second – and undoubtedly with far more radical implications – there has been a growing recognition that diversity issues are increasingly exceeding and surpassing the policy capacities of national governments and institutions.
>
> (Robins, 2007, p. 149)

Conclusion

This chapter has explored some of the key concepts that link to how (super)diversity is lived, understood, managed and reflected in media policy. The chapter made the distinction between living multi-culture and multiculturalism – policies and strategies – for managing the co-existence of diverse cultural and ethnic groups. It is important to keep in mind that multiculturalism has its roots in specific historical struggles – those linked to de-colonization and anti-racism – as well as ethnic revival, and it has striven to introduce new models of democratic citizenship that would replace exclusion and hierarchy. The shift from multiculturalism to civic integration in the 1990s has been politicized and politicians – including the UK Prime Minister David Cameron in 2011 – have framed the related debates around social cohesion and a unitary national culture, which in turn raises questions about how open it is and what is expected of 'others' if they are to integrate into it. The chapter has also discussed the undemocratic nature of the assimilationist policies that preceded multiculturalism ones and suggested that the re-emergence of 'new' assimilationism in some policies that claim to be integrationist needs to be taken seriously if inclusionary goals are to be achieved. The final section of the chapter discussed the place of diversity within media policy. It has suggested that policy making is not necessarily a neutral, detached, technical process but rather one in which political preferences come to the fore and some issues may be more politicized than others, and in such cases expertise may become more politicized and policies can change with changes in political power. Diversity is relevant for media policy makers because media can reflect different voices in society, they can give access to these voices and they can produce a range of contents that serve various groups in society. These broadly conceived dimensions of diversity are translated into rationales that underpin media regulation and policy. Three of these have been discussed in this chapter – effective communication, political diversity and cultural diversity. The chapter has also suggested that diversity-related goals can be set within a competition-focussed media regulatory environment (such as in the United States) or within a media environment with a public service broadcasting tradition that is closely related to diversity goals. It is this public service tradition and its relationship to media diversity that is discussed in Chapter 2.

2 Media Diversity and the Public Service Tradition

At the beginning of 2014 a United States federal court struck down the Federal Communication Commission's (FCC) 2010 Open Internet Order and prompted the so-called battle for true net neutrality. The FCC had introduced the order amid fears that internet service providers (ISPs) (some of the most successful ones being major cable companies such as Comcast, Time Warner and Verizon) could charge content providers (companies such as Netflix, Facebook or Vimeo) to deliver data to their customers through a so-called internet fast lane and hence create a two-tier internet. The FCC's order aimed to guarantee transparency and prohibit ISPs from blocking and unreasonable discrimination. However, following the court decision the regulator had to reconsider its approach. By the time it officially introduced its proposed new rules in May 2014, public interest in the topic had become huge, with rallies in major US cities supporting net neutrality and calling for a strong regulatory commitment to it. The FCC's servers crashed because of the number of public comments on the proposal and the Commission even took the unprecedented step of extending its public consultation deadline by three days, resulting in a record-breaking 3.7 million comments. The 'battle for true net neutrality' also included an internet slowdown day on 2 September 2014 with a number of online companies (including Netflix, Kickstarter, Etsy and Tumblr) carrying a graphic warning about what a two-tier internet will look like. The issues at stake in the new rules on net neutrality illustrate well how media and the broader communications industries play very special roles in our societies.

The campaigning organization Free Press launched its Save the Internet campaign arguing that:

> Our rights to connect and communicate – via universally accessible, open, affordable and fast communication networks and devices – are essential to our individual, economic and political freedoms.

The Internet is the foremost battleground for free speech in the 21st century, and protecting our Internet freedom is essential to safeguarding our rights to speak and assemble in private.

(Save the Internet, 2015)

US Senator Chuck Schumer argued for creating true net neutrality by re-classifying broadband providers as public utility companies: 'The internet in the 21st Century is as important to our future as highways were in the 20th Century. ... Like a highway, the internet must remain free and open for all; not determined by the highest bidders' (Sledge, 2014). In February 2015 the FCC indeed reclassified broadband internet as a public utility under Title II of the Communications Act, with President Obama vocally supporting such a move. This meant that FCC would treat providers of internet services similarly to providers of electricity, broadcast or mobile services. They are explicitly prohibited from blocking, throttling or prioritizing internet traffic for commercial reasons with the underlying rationale being that effective communication requires unobstructed access to channels of communication. The decision, however, did not mean that the FCC could intervene in pricing, network unbundling or technical operating requirements. At the time of writing (November 2015) lawsuits attacking the FCC's net neutrality rules were widely expected and it was not possible to predict whether and how their shape would evolve. However, the new rules are also important because regulatory trends are often set by the United States and the European Commission has been debating net neutrality rules for some time. It is also important to note here that the net neutrality rules are an example of regulation of the internet in the public interest, a rare occurrence because, in comparison to broadcasting, the internet tends to be significantly less regulated.

Public service broadcasting

The public discussions surrounding the 'battle for net neutrality' introduced stances that were reminiscent of earlier discussions about the nature of telecommunication services. These have been understood as businesses 'affected with a public interest' (Melody in McQuail, 1992, p. 21) due to the essential nature of the service, its tendency to monopoly and the requirement for universal accessibility. The problem of defining public interest in communication has been discussed widely. McQuail (1992) argues that difficulties arise through misunderstandings about which features of mass communication are essential and whether interferences with free market mechanisms are justified in order to secure these (see Chapter 3 in particular). He proposes that broadcasting in the public interest should guarantee universally accessible quality service, diversity as well as national political and/or cultural interest. In the UK broadcasting was from the onset considered to be a public good because of the limited nature of the broadcasting spectrum. A public good can be defined as:

> An item whose consumption is not decided by the individual but by the society as a whole, and which is financed by taxation.
>
> A public good (or service) may be consumed without reducing the amount available for others, and cannot be withheld from those who do not pay for it. Public goods (and services) include economic statistics and other information, law enforcement, national defense, parks, and other things for the use and benefit of all. No market exists for such goods, and they are provided to everyone by governments.
>
> (Business Dictionary, 2015)

In contrast, the approach that prevailed in the United States acknowledged that 'the commercial potential of broadcasting is clear and in some countries such as the US has been acknowledged from the earliest days of radio' (Feintuck and Varney, 2006, p. 41; see also McKenna, 2000). Robert McChesney (2004) argues that the commercial model was established gradually. At the beginning there existed non-profit radio broadcasting and there was a slow realization that profit could be generated from establishing national chains of stations that were supported by the sale of advertising. In Europe the understanding of broadcasting as a public good was also underpinned by a series of philosophical and political arguments. Among these was the need for a channel that provided information for citizens and a forum for discussion which enabled full participation in the political process.

> Off-air broadcasting has always been classified as a public good in the lexicon of economics, since unlike a commodity such as a cinema seat, access is potentially universal and everyone can enjoy it at the same time without interfering with anyone else. As we have seen however, from the outset public broadcasting was also thought out of as a 'public good' in a more general, philosophical sense, as an activity that aimed to contribute to the quality of communal life

and the development of democratic culture. Although other publicly funded institutions shared this ideal the limits imposed on them by space and location prevented them from matching broadcasting's universality.

(Murdock, 2004)

This understanding led to the establishment of public service broadcasting, in the UK embodied by the BBC (British Broadcasting Corporation). Although public broadcasting became established in the US, it 'has never aspired to emulate the European public service broadcasting model in which political and civic rather than economic relationships dominate. ... In particular, U.S. public broadcasting is a niche service ... not a comprehensive service as in some European countries' (Aufderheide, 1996, p. 63). According to Stuart Hall the public service idea clearly had its basis in the claim that there is 'such a thing as "the public interest" – a *social interest* – at stake in broadcasting' (1993, p. 24, original emphasis). He goes on to identify some of the roles of broadcasting in modern societies (source of knowledge, creator of a discursive space, a key pass between 'the governed' and 'the governors') and to argue that 'access to broadcasting has thus become a condition, a *sine qua non*, of modern citizenship' (ibid., p. 25). 'The public service philosophy of broadcasting ... is oriented towards the accessibility of pluralistic information for citizens and society rather than the freedom of communicators. Diversity of program content, accessible to all segments of the audience must be established and safeguarded' (Hoffman-Riem as quoted in McQuail, 1992, p. 142). Public service broadcasting thus takes into account that we are not only consumers but also citizens living in democratic societies who have a right to be adequately informed about matters of public importance. James Curran argues that this right is best guaranteed by public service broadcasting because 'it gives due attention to public affairs, and is less dominated by drama and entertainment than market-based broadcasting generally is' (1998, p. 190). A comparative study of television systems found this focus on news and current affairs to result in 'higher levels of political information in [European] nightly TV programs and foster greater knowledge of public affairs among viewers. The more market-driven and entertainment-centred television system of the United States, on the other hand, was shown to offer smaller amounts of hard news and to trigger less awareness of public affairs in the audience' (Esser et al., 2012, p. 248).

The ideal of public service broadcasting is closely linked to the concept of a mediated public sphere, the foundations of which were laid by Jürgen Habermas in his seminal study *The Structural Transformation of the Public Sphere*. Habermas' work has been widely discussed and critically assessed (see for example Garnham, 1990; Dahlgren, 1991; Fraser, 1993; Negt and Kluge, 1993; Robbins, 1993; Calhoun, 1997; Emden and Midgley, 2012). It remains crucial in analyzing contemporary media and their roles in democratic societies and the following provides a brief summary of some of the main points that are relevant to the discussion in this chapter. In his historical narrative Habermas identifies the peak of the bourgeois public sphere in the early to mid-19th century and characterizes it as a space in which private individuals came together as a public to use their own reason to discuss matters of public importance (for example, the power and direction of the state). Institutions of civil society – such as newspapers, debating societies, salons and coffee houses – were created as competitive market capitalism developed and these occupied a space distinct from both the economy and the state. However, the rational-critical debate that characterized the bourgeois public sphere at its peak declined with the further development of capitalism in the later 19th century and Habermas argues that the public sphere underwent such significant and detrimental changes that it continues to exist in appearance only. This brief summary of Habermas' arguments does not aim to provide a full account of his thesis, but to draw attention to the role that Habermas attributed to mass media in the disintegration of the public sphere. He identifies a particular problem which is a consequence of the conflation of journalism and literature and results in conjuring a peculiar reality, even a conflation of different levels of reality: 'instead of doing justice to reality, [journalism] has a tendency to present a substitute more palatable for consumption and more likely to give rise to an impersonal indulgence in stimulating relaxation than to a public use of reason' (1989, p. 170). However bleak this picture may seem in the case of the press, it was to get worse with the emergence of radio and television.

> With the arrival of new media [radio and television] the form of communication as such has changed; they have had an impact, therefore, more penetrating (in the strict sense of the word) than was ever possible for the press. Under the pressure of the 'Don't talk back!' the conduct of the public assumes a different form. In comparison with printed communications the programs sent by the new media curtail the reactions of their recipients in a peculiar way. They draw the eyes and ears of the public under their spell but at

the same time, by taking away its distance, place it under 'tutelage,' which is to say they deprive it of the opportunity to say something and to disagree. The critical discussion of the reading public tends to give way to 'exchanges about tastes and preferences' between consumers – even the talk about what is consumed, 'the examination of tastes,' becomes part of consumption itself.

(ibid., p. 171)

In more concrete terms Habermas identified the degree of economic concentration and technological-organizational co-ordination in media as a threat to the critical functions of publicist institutions.

For the arguments in this chapter three aspects of Habermas' theory – as discussed by Nicholas Garnham – are particularly important: the stress on 'the indissoluble link between the institutions and practices of mass communication and the institutions and practices of democratic societies'; the 'necessary material resource base for any public sphere' and finally the avoidance of the simple dichotomy of free market versus state control as threats to democracy can arise from both (1990, p. 360). It is also important to stress that, although news and current affairs programming tend to be readily associated with the democratic roles of media, television drama and factual entertainment play an equally important part in this respect. In his reappraisal of the democratic value of entertainment James Curran (2010) suggests that the three standard responses to the rise of media entertainment – treating it as a diversion from the serious democratic role of media; viewing it as separate from news and current affairs and finally focusing on entertainment with explicitly political contents – are all inadequate. Rather, he argues, there are four ways in which entertainment connects to the democratic life of society:

It provides a space for exploring and debating social values, which occupy a central place in contemporary politics. It offers a means of defining and refashioning social identity, something that is inextricably linked to a sense of self-interest. It affords alternative frameworks which inform public debate or ... a catalyst. And it provides a way of assessing, strengthening, weakening, and revising public norms that are an integral part of the way we govern ourselves.

(ibid., p. 85)

Academics are not the only ones who have failed to associate democratic values with entertainment that does not deal explicitly with political contents. It seems that this connection has been completely off the radar of policy makers. The failure of the international community (represented by the Office of the High Representative, the Organization for Security and Co-operation in Europe and the European Commission) to establish public service broadcasting in Bosnia Herzegovina in the aftermath of the 1995 Dayton Peace Agreement despite an investment of US$20 million was partly due to the fact that they 'failed ... to recognize the persistently important link between entertainment and politics in former Yugoslavia, and infused a fear of politics to such a degree that news and even election coverage [became] "politically neutered"' (Hozic, 2008, p. 151).

Public service broadcasting, national culture and minorities

Apart from contributing to political diversity, public service broadcasting has also been ascribed a role in building and safeguarding national culture, and hence its function in promoting cultural diversity should be considered. Public service broadcasting was established as a national institution that has played a role in constructing a national culture and, as mentioned in the Introduction, media policy and regulation can incorporate contradictory normative ideals. In this case the maintenance of a national culture into which the various groups in society are integrated can contradict the desire for diversity of voices and representations in the public sphere.

> In looking at the role of the media in creating a certain uniformity within the nation-state, we are in essence looking at the process of nation-building, and at how the media are consciously brought into play to construct a 'national' culture and a 'national' community. Nation-states must have a measure of common culture and civic ideology, a set of common understandings and aspirations, sentiments and ideas that bind the population together in their homeland.
>
> (Smith as quoted in van den Bulck, 2001, p. 54)

This focus on national culture is problematized in the context of the ethnic and cultural diversity (indeed superdiversity in some cases as suggested in Chapter 1) that characterizes contemporary societies. The increasingly diverse cultural identities lead to 'consequent pluralisation of cultural authority, which makes it increasingly difficult for broadcasters to see society as "a public" at all or to speak to it as if it were still part of a homogeneous, unified national culture' (Hall, 1993, p. 28). Hall goes on to argue that:

> Broadcasting ... has a major role – perhaps the critical role – to play in this 're-imagining of the nation': not by seeking to reimpose a unity and homogeneity which has long since departed, but by becoming the open space, the 'theatre' in which cultural diversity is produced, displayed and represented, and the 'forum' in which the terms of its associative life together are negotiated. ... This cultural negotiation about the terms on which the centralised culture of the nation can be reconstituted on more openly pluralistic lines remains broadcasting's key public cultural role – and one which cannot be sustained unless there is a public service idea and a system shaped in part by public service objectives to sustain it.
>
> (ibid., pp. 36–7)

In the 2010s – the age of on-demand online content – it may seem pointless to explore whether public service broadcasting plays a role in promoting cultural diversity. (It might be more accurate to refer to public service media, a term that reflects the changing nature of the provision and consumption of mediated contents; see, for example, Horsti et al., 2014.) However, we should keep in mind that public service offerings are based on particular normative ideals that are not associated with for-profit media as I argue further in Chapter 3.

In terms of cultural diversity as a rationale for media regulation, we need to keep in mind that public service broadcasters are regulated in ways that aim to ensure that their programming caters for the needs and interests of minority groups. (The licensing of commercial broadcasters differs significantly in this respect.) This can be in the form of specific programmes (or channels) in minority languages or the requirement to reflect the range of cultures, opinions and so on that characterize the society at large, which applies across all public service channels, as in the case of the BBC. In McQuail's (1992a) terminology this corresponds to a high degree of internal diversity, with the needs of various groups in society being met by a large range of programmes on the same channel. However, arguments relating to the role of public service media in nation building or the promotion of coherence should not only address the issue of inclusion in the mediated nation but also the crucial question of exclusion (Cole, 1998). As mentioned in Chapter 1 Fraser's (1993) argument about public discursive arenas as sites in which the construction of social identities occurs is highly pertinent when we explore questions of inclusion and exclusion.

The ways in which social and cultural identities have been constructed in public service programming have been the subject of scrutiny also. The BBC, for example, has faced criticism for its elitist attitude to raising the cultural standards of the 'masses', Raymond Williams has been particularly critical of the elitist approaches according to which the 'masses' influenced high culture in undesirable ways. He summarized the elitist argument in a series of questions:

> Isn't there great danger of the tradition of high culture being overwhelmed by mass culture, which expresses the tastes and standards of the ordinary man? Isn't really our first duty to defend minority culture, which in its actual works is the highest achievement of humanity?
>
> (Williams as quoted in O'Connor, 2006, p. 19)

The BBC's shift to more popular programming has in some cases represented a response to political problems, Anthony McNicholas (2004) argues that this was the case in the 1980s when the launch of the soap opera *EastEnders* was to address 'the loss of audience share to the commercial companies, particularly by BBC1; the changing nature of television schedules and a general perception that the corporation was an elite institution which was out of touch with the viewing (and crucially, licence fee paying) public' (p. 491). The BBC's focus on catering for the needs of the majority ethnic group has been scrutinized repeatedly. In 2001 its then Director General Greg Dyke labelled the BBC 'hideously white', a criticism that continues to resurface. For example, in March 2015 the BBC Trust – the BBC's governing body – criticized Radio 2 for being 'too white', with its reach remaining considerably lower than average among black, Asian and minority ethnic audiences. In this context it is worth mentioning that public service broadcasters face complex challenges in relation to the transnationalization of media and media audiences, as discussed in Chapter 4.

Minorities are also served by media specifically aimed at them and these can be commercial or not-for-profit ones. Although they are not necessarily linked to the public service broadcasting tradition, it is important to briefly discuss them here. The most important issue to remember is that minority media tend to be marginalized, and some are particularly fragile because they fall outside the framework of nation-states within which the given minority could make claims to access to the media in democratic societies. The case of the Roma – Europe's largest transnational ethnic minority group – and the marginalization of their media are particularly telling in this respect. (See Metykova, 2015 on the complex roles played by the Roma media in the Czech Republic as mediators between the Roma minority and the Czech majority.) The roles of minority media vary but their primary aim is to celebrate the culture of the given minority, while other goals include the preservation and advancement of a minority language as well as the combating of negative stereotypes that appear in mainstream media. In some cases minority media promote links with countries of origin and may also support political (and/or social) change in those. Some minority media involve co-operation between minorities and majorities, and they target a variety of audiences, often including the majority, and may seek to increase social inclusion through their work, an aim that may be supported by government policies (see for example Browne, 2005). Charles Husband argues that media are 'a core element in civil society and a fundamental prerequisite for the promotion of civic trust in complex multi-ethnic societies' (1998, p. 136). He also considers that it is crucial for ethnic minority media to become part of the public sphere at the 'most encompassing level' so that they can participate in meaningful dialogue that affects cross community relationships in order to prevent the creation of parallel and exclusive public spheres (Husband, 2000). Concerns have indeed been raised about the possibility of minority media being 'isolated' or 'ghettoized' and it should also be mentioned that migrant or minority populations' use of media from their countries of origin is viewed by some as a sign of their unwillingness to integrate into their 'new' societies (for a critique of this stance see for example Christiansen, 2004; Aksoy and Robins, 2003; see also Chapter 4) rather than a way of dealing with the lack of media contents catering for their needs and interests.

In 2008 policy makers in EU countries formally recognized the role of community media and introduced policy tools to support them. Community media do not fall under the category of public service broadcasters but I have included them in the discussion because they are tasked with increasing social cohesion and are linked to some of the diversity rationales mentioned in Chapter 1. A 2008 resolution of the European Parliament acknowledges the 'role played by community media in promoting civic empowerment; enriching social debate; strengthening cultural and linguistic diversity, social inclusion and local identity, and facilitating the social integration of disadvantaged members of society and of all kinds of communities within society threatened with exclusion' (McGonagle, 2008–9). Community media (in the case of the UK, community radio to be precise), as their name suggests, are run by local communities or communities of shared interest, religion or ethnicity on a not-for-profit basis. They tend to rely on the work of volunteers and they target a general (local) audience or specific groups such as youth, ethnic minorities and religious communities. Importantly, 'community media are non-profit making and independent, not only from national, but also from local power, engaging primarily in activities of public and civil society interest, serving clearly defined objectives which always include social value and contribute to intercultural dialogue' (ibid.). According to a report by the UK's communications regulator Ofcom, as of 2014 a total of 215 analogue community radio stations were licensed to broadcast in the UK (Ofcom, 2014, p. 8). The policy rationales behind the support for community media are clearly linked to supporting diversity by providing access to communication to groups that may otherwise be excluded and also by supporting a wider range of voices and opinions in contents.

Marketization and changes in public service broadcasting

As already mentioned, Habermas' exploration of the public sphere also stresses its material base. Some relevant principles of public service broadcasting in this respect include 'distance from vested interests; direct funding and universality of payment; competition in good programming rather than for numbers; and guidelines that liberate rather than restrict programme makers' (Broadcasting Research Unit as quoted in Raboy, 1996, p. 6). The ways in which public service broadcasting is funded impact on the distance from vested interests (or independence from the state as well as from the market) and on efforts at maximizing audience size which may be detrimental to the quality of programming. Siune and Hultén point out that one of the defining features of public broadcasting in Europe is 'an element of public finance' (1998, p. 24), referring to the fact that some public service broadcasters are allowed to generate commercial income, which raises the question of whether it is in line with their mission. (Those who subscribe to the 'purist' stance argue that public service broadcasters should not be involved in any commercial activities while 'pragmatists' believe that these are not incompatible with the public service rationale, see for example Raboy, 1996; Blumler, 1993.) In any case, there appears to be agreement that funding arrangements for public service broadcasting need to be transparent and not tied to competition for audiences, and the broadcasters must be accountable to the public.

Public service broadcasters are, however, not the only players on media markets. For example, in the UK commercial television broadcasting was introduced in 1955, while some European countries introduced commercial broadcasting considerably later – the Netherlands in the late 1980s – and post-communist countries such as Poland, the Czech Republic and Hungary established a broadcasting duopoly when transforming their state controlled media system in the late 1980s/early 1990s.

> The arrival of ITV, though seen as revolutionary and clearly a severe threat to the BBC's domination of broadcasting, in the longer term resulted only in a power-sharing arrangement, with public-service values coexisting reasonably happily with the degree of commercialism introduced. As recently as 1981, before the advent of Channel 4, television in Britain was still in effect a comfortable duopoly, with power shared between BBC and the ITV companies. In the years since then, however, a fifth terrestrial channel has come on-stream, and much more significantly, new technologies, including cable, digital terrestrial and especially direct-to-home (DTH) satellite broadcasting, have changed the nature of British television.
>
> (Feintuck and Varney, 2006, p. 2)

Although the UK television environment has undergone significant changes since the 1980s (the most recent emergence of companies that specialize in on-demand content is, for example, discussed in Chapter 3), the basic distinction between broadcasters that have been granted a public service remit and those with a clear for-profit agenda continues to be relevant.

Discussions about the societal roles of broadcasting have not been new and some of the insights from previous decades continue to be relevant not only for academic explorations but also when determining policy goals. Writing in 1974, Raymond Williams made an insightful prediction about the possible developments that television – and other communication-related technologies – faced and his thoughts are worth quoting at length:

> Over a wide range from general television through commercial advertising to centralised information and data-processing systems, the technology that is now or is becoming available can be used

to affect, to alter, and in some cases to control our whole social process. And it is ironic that the uses offer such extreme social choices. We could have inexpensive, locally based yet internationally extended television systems, making possible communication and information-sharing on a scale that not long ago would have seemed utopian. These are the contemporary tools of the long revolution towards an educated and participatory democracy, and of the recovery of effective communication in complex urban and industrial societies. But they are also the tools of what would be, in context, a short and successful counter-revolution, in which, under cover of talk about choice and competition, a few para-national corporations, with their attendant states and agencies, could further reach into our lives, at every level from news to psycho-drama, until individual and collective response to many different kinds of experience and problem became almost limited to choice between their programmed possibilities.

(p. 151)

Despite technological developments that arguably enhance the potential of television in communication and information-sharing for democratic purposes, Williams' vision has not materialized.

The political-economic trend in Europe in the 1980s can be characterized as a liberalization of markets in general.

Liberalisation introduced competition into broadcast markets that were previously either public monopolies (as in most western European countries) or duopolies with strong public service regulation, as in Britain. ... As well as massively enlarging their sphere of action private television interests also succeeded in winning more space for manoeuvre by pressing for the rules governing ownership and advertising to be relaxed and getting the underlying purpose of regulation redefined.

(Murdock, 2004)

Policy changes that accompanied this liberalizing trend have been widely explored (see for example Murdock, 1990 and McChesney, 2004) and characterized as deregulation (see Chapter 3) by some, although Murdock (1997) points out that deregulation is a misnomer and we should rather discuss these developments as re-regulation. David Hesmondhalgh prefers the term 'marketization' to describe the policy changes that have been ongoing since the 1980s. He refers to Slater and Tonkiss' characterization of marketization as 'the permeation of market exchange as a social principle', a process that has been ongoing for centuries and as a result 'in modern capitalist societies, market and non-market relations coexist, but market relations dominate in terms of how society is coordinated and organised' (Hesmondhalgh, 2013, p. 128). Hesmondhalgh also uses the term to describe three significant processes that impacted on cultural industries:

the *privatisation* of government-owned enterprises and institutions, many of which were once privately owned; the *lifting of restraints* on the activities of businesses so that they could pursue profit more easily, often at the expense of other considerations, such as serving and informing publics; the *expansion of private ownership* as a result, together with other changes in the law and regulation that allow this to occur.

(ibid., p. 128, original emphasis)

These processes had a significant impact on public service broadcasting.

In the case of the UK, John Keane (1991) argues that there are three principal reasons for the decline of public service broadcasting (understood as a decline in the quality of public service broadcasting as well as a decline in the number of viewers/listeners): fiscal squeeze, legitimacy problems and technological change. Nicholas Garnham suggests that public service broadcasting is characterized by a 'failure sufficiently to distinguish between two communicative functions within the public sphere: the collection and dissemination of *information*, and the provision of a forum for *debate*' (1990, p.111, original emphasis), while Graham Murdock thinks that the public broadcasting system failed to 'keep pace with the proliferation of political and social discourses, [and] produced a crisis in the relations between public broadcasting and the viewer-as-citizen ... [which was] exacerbated by the increasing tension between broadcasters, state agencies and government' (1992, p. 31). Marc Raboy also alerts us to the role of the larger political framework when he suggests that 'problems of financing, mandate, and interpretations of purpose are all indications of a more fundamental problem of political will' (1996, p. 2). He goes on to argue that in relation to the broader policy framework 'the principal normative question will remain: What should be the public function of broadcasting in a democracy?' (ibid., p. 4).

Public service broadcasting from multiculturalism to diversity and beyond

When considering changes to public service broadcasting in relation to the focus of this book – diversity – it is important to explore how the shift from multiculturalism to integration (as discussed in Chapter 1) was translated into policies and regulations related to public service broadcasting. As already suggested multiculturalist strategies developed by European governments targeted specific ethnic groups for inclusion, and this was also reflected in policies related to media.

> [In the UK] multicultural broadcasting policies (most notably between the 1970s following the UK Race Relations Acts and up until the 1990 Broadcasting Act) included recruitment measures, targets and specialist slots and multicultural departments (or in the case of the BBC, separate African-Caribbean and Asian Programmes Units for a period in the 1990s), designed to explicitly position Black and Asian representation on the media agenda. As part of a broader regime of cultural governance, Channel 4 also positively acknowledged UK multiculture in both representation and structure. Its true innovation was as the only UK terrestrial channel established (in 1982) with multicultural programming embedded as part of its core practice and infrastructure. This direct engagement with questions of representation and racial stereotyping implied an interventionist politics predicated on anti-racism within an early idea of state multiculturalism.
>
> (Malik, 2013, p. 232)

Awad and Roth discuss the approach of the Dutch public service broadcaster to the provision of programmes for ethnic minority groups which was very different from the UK one. This was partly because of the different way in which Dutch public service broadcasting is organized, with channels or blocks of time allocated to various interest groups within society (see for example Brants and McQuail, 1997), so that between the 1960s and 1980s programmes were produced for specific minority groups in their own languages. Awad and Roth go on to argue that the approach was beneficial because it addressed the exclusionary effects of the dominant public sphere (that is, the public sphere associated with mainstream media) and created spaces 'for minority groups to define and articulate their social perspective;

develop alternative discourses and styles of communication; and raise their voices against injustice' (2011, p. 403).

A German example of a multicultural public service radio station – Radio Multikulti that broadcast in Berlin between 1994 and 2008 – has been discussed not only in relation to national policies but particularly as a city-based example of a multicultural mediated space. The radio station broadcast in a number of different languages and Vertovec (1996) argues that it attempted to break down Germany's conceptualizations of 'foreignness' in its attempt to address immigrants (and the indigenous population) as Berliners.

> World-music, featuring everything except Anglo-American music, afternoons and evenings given to foreign-language programmes in about 18 different languages, and German-language programmes lasting into the afternoon which report on 'multicultural' life in the city are the major elements through which the idea of 'integrative' broadcasting is put into practice. ... The idea is to address immigrants primarily as Berliners, that is, as members of a local community to which they belong regardless of citizenship. Their ambitious effort to combine broadcasting *for* and *about* immigrants has been widely regarded as a success.
>
> (Kosnick, 2000, p. 335, original emphasis)

The radio station was closed down in 2008 on financial grounds and its frequency was taken over by Funkhaus Europa which – as the name suggests – has not maintained its city-based character.

Changes to multicultural programming occurred in the late 1990s in a number of European countries (see for example Horsti and Hultén, 2011 on Sweden and Finland; Titley, 2014 for an overview of changes in European public service broadcasting). In the Netherlands programmes aimed specifically at minority populations were discontinued and an overall approach was adopted which offered cross-cultural programming – in the Dutch language, aimed at a much broader audience (and hence being more competitive) and attempting to attract immigrants' descendants in particular – first at national and then at local levels. This move was in line with the wider policy of integration which – as discussed in Chapter 1 – can have assimilationist elements. The overall shift from multiculturalism to integration manifested itself in UK public service broadcasting at the beginning of the 2000s:

The BBC and Channel 4 reformulated their multicultural depart-
ments and promoted (through programming, policy, and address)
a more mainstream definition of cultural diversity ... that was, in
turn, to pave the way for creative diversity. The significance of these
important acknowledgements of structural inequalities, discrimination, and cultural representation is that they are all trumped by a
bigger emphasis on a socially broad conception of 'cultural diversity'
and apparently inclusive way of managing diversity.

(Malik, 2013, p. 232; see also Garnham, 2005)

The shift away from multiculturalist approaches to public service
broadcasting is linked to broader changes in the industry (the already
discussed marketization) and to socio-political factors. Some of these
relate to audience fragmentation and the changing demographic make-
up of European societies which cannot be ignored in media policy.
However, as Awad and Roth argue:

[W]hile the changing nature of minorities' media needs may be
obvious, it is less obvious what those needs are. Defining them is a
political decision rather than the natural consequence of changing
demographics. It is a decision tied to certain assumptions about the
media's power in shaping a culturally diverse society and about the
specific shape that such a society should take.

(Awad and Roth, 2011, pp. 410–11)

Importantly, as Malik indicates:

[W]hat these creative diversity scripts start to tell us about updated
principles of public service, branding, and accountability is that
quality and creativity are now foregrounded over (structural) questions of (in)equality. Human resources becomes more important
than content, and a broad sense of diversity is promoted rather
than the naming of specific communities. Furthermore, the ubiq-
uitous creative diversity paradigm is shaped by a pro-creative
agenda and openly *not* by a politics of recognition of social or
cultural difference.

(2013, p. 236, original emphasis)

This, as suggested in Chapter 1, is related to the de-ethnicization of difference and the discourse of post-race.

New media and diversity of access

The emergence of new media technologies raises a number of relevant questions in relation to diversity. The opening of this chapter highlighted some issues of access to online channels of communication (for new media and diversity of contents see Chapter 6). However, concerns about uneven access were expressed soon after the introduction of the internet. Tod Gitlin, for example, argued that 'there is one problem which the new means of communication do not address and may even worsen: the existence of a two-tier society. To those who are information-rich (or information-glutted) shall more information be given' (1998, p. 172). It appears that gender, race and socio-economic status continue to be factors influencing access to and use of new media technologies, and that also in some of the most developed countries of the world. Celeste Campos-Castillo (2014) argues that while the uptake of the internet grew in the United States, those studying the digital divide turned their attention to questions of use. However, the question of access remains relevant even in developed countries like the US where in the period between 2007 and 2012 Whites were most likely to have internet access. In June 2015 the FCC advanced a proposal that would allow the government to subsidize broadband access for poor families, stating that:

> Broadband has become essential to participation in modern society, offering access to jobs, education, health care, government services and opportunity. Unfortunately, income remains a significant barrier to broadband adoption:
>
> - While over 95% of households with incomes of $150,000 or more have access, only 48% of those making less than $25,000 have service at home.
> - Low-income consumers disproportionately use smart phones for Internet access – but nearly 50% of them have had to cancel or suspend smartphone service due to financial hardship.
>
> (FCC, 2015b)

Feintuck and Varney point out that broadcasting has been more heavily regulated than the internet in the public interest, even in the US which does not have a tradition of public service broadcasting that is comparable to the European one. In US regulation the fact that the spectrum is in effect a 'public natural resource' has been used to justify regulatory intervention (see Chapter 3). In 2006, Feintuck and Varney observed that: 'To date, however, the information revolution, especially as manifested in the Internet, has not been claimed for the public, but has largely been left to the whim of its commercial developers and market forces' (p. 27). Their point resonated in 2014 when the so-called battle for net neutrality highlighted the potential dangers of commercial interests dominating access to and use of the internet (see Chapter 2). Indeed, policies related to new media tend to be guided by economic goals. For example, the roll-out of broadband tends to be conceptualized as part of regional economic development and, although policies may refer to the social benefits of broadband, these are not easy to detect and indeed analyses suggest that the most excluded groups in society do not benefit from them (see van Winden and Woets, 2004 for an overview; Dini et al., 2012; Katz, 2012). Explorations of inequalities in access to the internet have been supplemented with considerations about inequalities in digital skills and in usage of the internet. Working with a representative survey of the Dutch population van Deursen and van Dijk concluded that:

> As the Internet becomes more mature, its usage reflects traditional media use in society; Internet use increasingly reflects known social, economic and cultural relationships present in the offline world, including inequalities. ... The intensive and extensive nature of Internet use among the well-off and well-educated suggests an elite lifestyle from which those with less capital are marginalized. ... Although inequalities within society have always existed, the Internet created an even stronger division; the higher status members increasingly gain access to more information than the lower status members.
>
> (2014, p. 521)

Graham Murdock points out that access to the internet is only one issue when we consider its potential for social inclusion, political and cultural diversity.

> Taken together these technologies make it entirely possible to only watch what one already enjoys and to only encounter opinions one already agrees with. In a situation where worldviews are increasingly polarised and talking across differences on a basis of knowledge and respect is more vital than ever to a working deliberative system,

this hollowing out of collective space presents a major challenge to democratic culture.

(Murdock, 2004)

It does not come as a surprise that Habermas remains sceptical about the potential of the internet in building political public spheres:

Whereas the growth of systems and networks multiplies possible contacts and exchanges of information, it does not lead per se to the expansion of an intersubjectively shared world and to the discursive interweaving of conceptions of relevance, themes, and contradictions from which political public spheres arise. The consciousness of planning, communicating and acting subjects seems to have simultaneously expanded and fragmented. The publics produced by the Internet remain closed off from one another like global villages.

(Habermas quoted in Downey and Fenton, 2003, p. 189)

The fragmentation of the online audience and the creation of closed-off communities that do not engage with politics has been a concern for researchers in a variety of disciplines, and young people in particular have been the focus of studies on declining news consumption. Personalized internet filters allow users to stray away from information that they find irrelevant, hence they can be isolated from diverse news topics and sources, potentially polarizing the public sphere (see for example Beam and Kosicki, 2014). Like-minded individuals can easily create isolated enclaves and communicate in echo chambers (see for example Sunstein, 2009) or filter bubbles (Pariser, 2011).

More recent research, however, questions some of these assumptions. A 2014 survey of US millennials (young people aged 18 to 34) shows that keeping up with the news is at least somewhat important to 85 per cent of the respondents, 45 per cent of whom follow five or more 'hard news' stories (Media Insight Project, 2015). In their study of Dutch non-users of online and offline news Trilling and Schoenback argue that:

The civic duty to keep informed in general is still one of the strongest predictors for both using news overviews at all and the frequency of exposure. ... The Internet might have the potential to reach those who do not feel a strong civic duty to keep informed. On the Internet, people with weak civic attitudes actually seem to follow the news: regardless of how strong their civic attitudes, their preference for entertainment and their political interest are, their frequency of exposure does not differ.

(2012, p. 45)

Joseph Kahne et al. (2011) considered arguments about online communication spaces acting as an echo chamber as opposed to spaces with divergent political perspectives when exploring the online practices and civic and political engagement of US youth aged 16–21. They argue that discussions about the internet's influence on exposure to diverse civic and political perspectives should also pay attention to non-political online activity – echoing Curran's argument about the role that entertainment plays in our lives in democratic societies. They also state that studying mere exposure is insufficient, we need to understand how young people actually engage with diverse perspectives.

Conclusion

This chapter has argued that public service broadcasting – as established in European democratic societies – has been guided by an understanding of broadcasting as a public good and has been regulated in the public interest – despite problems with the lack of a clear definition of what constitutes public interest in communication. It has been underpinned by a philosophy that takes into account the importance of the communication needs of citizens living in a democratic society, and has been linked to the concept of a public sphere as developed by Habermas – a space which is separate from the state as well as the market. Public service broadcasting is also a national cultural institution and as such plays a significant role in the construction of national culture. It is tasked with contradictory normative ideals – the inclusion of a variety of voices and representations that reflect the major differences in society contrasts with a role in the integration (or increasingly the assimilation) of diverse voices. The role of public service media has been largely discussed in terms of a normative ideal in this chapter and I have considered some actual developments in contemporary societies (and their media) that complicate this role. The increased cultural diversity of contemporary societies and the fragmentation of audiences are two examples of such developments. Criticisms of public service broadcasters' insufficient opening-up to cultural minorities persist, although measures introduced as part of state multicultural-ism arguably contribute to a culturally more diverse workforce and programming. The shift to diversity (and creative diversity) policies in public service broadcasting is characterized by the mainstreaming of difference and its de-ethnicization which denies structural inequalities and discrimination. The chapter has also argued that with the increas-ing popularity of capitalist attitudes the public sphere underwent det-rimental changes. In the case of public service broadcasting these are linked to marketization (the introduction of commercial competitors on European media markets during the second half of the 20th cen-tury) and a crisis of legitimacy as well as socio-political changes. The last section of the chapter considered whether new media provide a ready-made solution to improving access to diverse channels of com-munication and whether they increase choice. (Their role in increasing the diversity of contents is considered in Chapter 6.) Despite the pro-claimed and empirically widely tested role of new media in empower-ing citizens, access continues to be divided along racial, gender and income lines, an issue that has been recognized by the US communica-tions regulator. It is, however, not only access but also the use of the internet that increasingly reflects the inequalities of the offline world. Although public service broadcasting has been in 'crisis' – the causes and manifestations of which are manifold – the chapter argues that the normative ideal that it embodies has not lost its relevance and the lack of political will to address the question of the role of media in a democ-racy in a sustainable manner is detrimental as market competition is not sufficient to ensure the democratic roles of media, an argument that I develop in the next chapter.

3 Media Diversity and the Marketplace of Ideas

Chapter 2 discussed public service broadcasting which has been under-stood to be closely related to democratic citizenship and diversity. The chapter suggested that public service broadcasting as a normative ideal has addressed issues of inclusion and representation in the mediated public sphere, but with the fragmentation of audiences, marketization, legitimacy crisis and technological change, it has become increasingly difficult to fulfil its ideal roles. This, however, does not mean that the roles that public service broadcasting has been intended (and regu-lated) to play can easily be transferred to commercial media players or that the emergence of new media technologies makes these normative ideals redundant. Chapter 2 discussed special regulatory arrangements that apply to public service broadcasting, particularly in relation to minority groups, that are closely linked to political and cultural diver-sity and that are – to a decreasing extent – sheltered from market com-petition. The central aim of this chapter is to explore some of the key debates on market competition as a means of ensuring media diversity. It discusses some of the key economic characteristics of the media in order to set the parameters of the debate and then it moves on to con-sider whether market competition is an effective mechanism for the promotion of a diversity of media players and whether the emergence of new media technologies alleviates some aspect of market failure.

In 1984 the top US media regulator Mark Fowler (then chairman of the FCC) compared television to a toaster with pictures and argued that it needed no more government regulation than an electrical appli-ance (Miller, 2007). The previous chapters have clarified that media cannot be treated like other consumer products in that they play social, cultural as well as political roles. However, Fowler's argument was not flawed for this reason alone. Although media are subject to standard economic and financial forces, when interpreting these one must recognize how media differ from other products and services (Picard, 2005). Chapter 2 argues that media are affected by public interest because of the essential nature of the service that they provide and because the service must be universally accessible. It also showed that (some) media outputs are crucial for maintaining an informed citizenry, a shared culture and also for debating socially significant issues. 'There are some forms of content that are collectively desirable and that everyone benefits from (e.g. documentaries, educational and cultural programmes) but which viewers, on an individual basis, might not tune into or be prepared to pay for' (Doyle, 2005, p. 66); such contents are considered merit goods by economists. This chapter considers the role of market-driven approaches and advertising as a key funding mechanism within the context of a diverse media diet that citizens (as opposed to consumers) benefit from.

The final part of the chapter focusses on broader policy developments, mainly the trend towards deregulation – the removal of government regulatory controls – that has perhaps been most significant in the case of the US but has also been adopted by policy makers in many European countries. One consequence of deregulatory measures has been a decrease in the number of media that control a large share of a market, for example, 90 per cent of US media was owned by 50 companies in 1983, in 2011 the same share of US media was owned by only six companies (Lutz, 2012). Concerns about media concentration and its impact not only on the diversity of media players in a particular market but also on the quality of democratic debate have long been raised by media scholars and researchers, but they have also become the subject of grassroots campaigns on a national basis (such as the Media Reform Coalition in the UK) and at the transnational level (such as the European Initiative for Media Pluralism).

The marketplace of ideas

It has already been argued that one dimension of diversity that informs media policy is effective communication, which is linked to the freedom of speech ideal. A good starting point for discussing the role of market competition in ensuring these freedoms is the case of the United States, where the metaphor of the marketplace of ideas has been used to justify the first amendments of freedom of speech and freedom of press.

Although this classic image of competing ideas and robust debate dates back to English philosophers John Milton and John Stuart

Mill, Justice Holmes first introduced the concept into American jurisprudence in his 1919 dissent to Abrams v. United States: 'the best test of truth is the power of thought to get itself accepted in the competition of the market'. This theory assumes that a process of robust debate, if uninhibited by governmental interference, will lead to the discovery of truth, or at least the best perspectives or solutions for societal problems. A properly functioning marketplace of ideas, in Holmes's perspective, ultimately assures the proper evolution of society, wherever that evolution might lead.

(Ingber, 1986, p. 3)

The marketplace of ideas has been scrutinized extensively since 1919 and in the 1940s the predecessor of the Federal Communications Commission (FCC) attempted to address some of its limitations with its Fairness Doctrine:

Broadcasters must provide time, free of charge if necessary, for the coverage of controversial issues of public importance and for the presentation of contrasting views concerning such issues. Furthermore, individuals personally attacked during a broadcast on these issues are entitled to 'reply time' so they can broadcast a response to the attack.

(ibid., pp. 57–8)

The development of the Fairness Doctrine was linked to the expectation that the limitations of the broadcast spectrum might hinder the functioning of the marketplace of ideas and to the introduction of the licensing of broadcast frequencies:

Chaos had resulted before 1927 when the allocation of frequencies was left entirely to the private sector. Congress wrote the Radio Act of 1927 to recognize the air waves as a public domain and to provide for government licensing of their use according to the public interest, convenience, and necessity.

(Swegman Brundage, 1972, p. 531)

It is thus clear that the introduction and spread of broadcasting in the United States prompted a different regulatory response from the one discussed in Chapter 2, but it also became evident to US policy makers that interventions in market competition might be necessary to ensure the diversity of views and topics in the media.

In subsequent decades calls for reforming the media market continued: a *Harvard Law Review* article written by Jerome Barron in 1967 and entitled 'Access to the Press – A New First Amendment Right' attained iconic status. 'Developed against the egalitarian background and political turmoil of the 1960s, and reflecting a growing awareness of the threat posed by media consolidation to a diverse "marketplace" of information and ideas, Barron's article ambitiously proposed a constitutional right of public access not only to broadcast, but to print media' (Heins and Freedman, 2007, p. 917). Des Freedman outlines the key limitations of instruments linked to the freedoms of speech and press, and argues that the degree to which these policy instruments were guarantors of such freedoms has been exaggerated: 'according to media historian Paul Starr, the First Amendment was scarred by the political tension of the time in which it was drafted' (2008, p. 59). We should also bear in mind that these instruments were developed in a radically different media environment. 'Today, however, the western media is characterized by transnational corporations, oligopolistic markets, literate audiences and fierce competition for revenue. ... More recent interpretations of phenomena such as the First Amendment and the "marketplace of ideas" metaphor are misleading in that they are often the result of a highly contemporary and inflexible attachment to the desirability of market forces that was lacking in the original formulations' (ibid., pp. 60–1).

The question of perfect competition

The brief description above has alluded to the fact that in the case of the United States ensuring freedom of speech and freedom of press was entrusted to market forces and the government was expected only to intervene in exceptional cases when competition was threatened: 'Fairness regulations presume that when a few individuals or groups control a critical medium, they will stifle competition of ideas and block the emergence of truth' (Ingber, 1984, p. 58). However, it has been argued convincingly that the premise that the free market involves no government intervention is false. 'All media systems are the result of explicit government policies, subsidies, grants of rights and regulations. ... Indeed, to have anything close to competitive markets in media requires extensive government regulation in the form of ownership limits and myriad other policies' (McChesney, 2003, p. 126). Gillian Doyle explains that '[p]erfect competition exists when there are many sellers of a good or a service that is homogeneous (i.e. exactly the same or not differentiated) and no firm(s) dominate(s) the market. In such a situation economic forces operate freely. ... It is very rare to find an example of perfect competition in the real world' (2002, p. 8). Rather, what we face is imperfect competition where:

> Cost advantages associated with size will dictate that an industry should be an oligopoly [when a particular market is controlled by a small number of companies] unless some form of market intervention or Government regulation prevents the firms from growing to their most efficient size. If no such intervention takes place, existing firms in the industry may create barriers to entry where natural ones do not exist so that the industry will be dominated by a handful of large firms only because they are successful in preventing the entry of new firms. But substantial economies of scale in any industry will, in themselves, act as a natural barrier to entry in that any new firms will usually be smaller than established firms and so they will be at a cost disadvantage.
>
> (ibid., p. 9)

This already suggests that without regulatory interventions competition may actually hinder the presence of a diversity of players on a market, an issue that is particularly pertinent in the case of the media as I explain further in this chapter.

There is another important fact about the media that we need to bear in mind. Media industries are particularly prone to market failure, a term that is normally used in two ways: to describe 'any failure by the market system to allocate resources efficiently' or to describe a 'failure of the market to advance socially desirable goals other than efficiency, such as preserving democracy and social cohesion' (Doyle, 2002, p. 64). Two consequences of failure in media markets are concentration – which I discussed briefly in the Introduction and will deal with in more detail later in the chapter – and externalities. In the words of the economist Milton Friedman, an externality is 'the effect of a transaction ... on a third party who has not consented to or played any role in the carrying out of that transaction' (as quoted in Bakan, 2004, p. 61). A frequently mentioned negative externality is pollution, while an example of a positive externality might be a playground which is freely accessible to all or a nice view. Edwin Baker (2002) insists that in order to assess whether media give their audiences what the audiences want we must take externalities into account. The areas that should be considered in this respect include the quality of public opinion and political participation; audience members' interactions with other people; audience members' impact on cultural products available to others; exposing and deterring abuses of power; other behavioural responses to the possibility of media exposure; non-paying recipients; positive benefits to people or entities wanting their message spread; messages' negative effects on those who do not want the attention; gains or losses to media sources; and costs imposed or benefits created by information-gathering techniques.

While Baker's is a comprehensive overview, other writers focus on selected externalities. For example, Mark Cooper stresses that '[t]he public at large benefits from the watchdog function beyond the value that individual media firms can capture in their market transactions (advertising revenue and viewer payments)' (2003, p. 42). Edward Herman (1997) compares externalities linked with commercial and public service broadcasting and argues that in respect of public affairs, cultural and children's programming (all of which can be sources of positive externalities) commercial media fail, and moreover they tend to exploit sex and violence which can result in negative externalities.

It is clear from this brief discussion that some externalities are beneficial and policy interventions could be designed to promote them within a competition framework. However, as Baker argues, there are difficulties with assessing and measuring externalities in the media context – such externalities often involve non-economic values (more informed citizens) and freedom of expression (preventing harm to others that is caused by broadcasting a message). Apart from the difficulty of measuring externalities, '[o]ften their significance, even their valence, is disputable. Therefore, whether any particular regime gives the audience what it wants will likewise be continually contestable. Although empirical information is helpful, the evaluation is inherently political' (Baker, 2002, p. 43). (The political nature of policy making is also discussed in Chapter 1.)

Some aspects of diversity understood as access to channels of communication have been discussed in earlier chapters. My focus in the context of the marketplace of ideas is on whether unrestricted competition leads to a greater diversity of players on a particular market, or in other words whether it ensures freedom of entry into the marketplace. To consider this question, we need to delve further into some of the economic characteristics of media. The so-called fixed costs (that is, costs that do not depend on the amount of goods produced, such as leasing a building or marketing costs) entailed in the creation of media outputs tend to be high. Media industries produce outputs that are characterized by a high degree of uncertainty in terms of consumer evaluation and by their uniqueness. There is an oversupply of media contents and since it is impossible to consume them all, consumers exercise significant power in determining the success and pricing of a product. It remains difficult to predict audience tastes despite the use of a variety of marketing strategies, including focus group discussions. High product failure rates are typical of media industries yet 'successes are well rewarded financially. In Hollywood, for example, 10 percent of the top 200 films typically account for 50% of industry revenue' (Picard, 2005, p. 67). Following the release of Disney's 2013 animated film *Frozen*, the UK media ran reports about parents desperately hunting down merchandise as retailers online and offline ran out of stocks quickly, and Disney admitted that it did not expect the film to be such a success. As of May 2014 the film had made over $1.2 billion worldwide and was heralded as the highest grossing animated film of all time. In addition, it gained critical acclaim, winning two Oscars in 2014, including for best animated feature film (Wood, 2014). It is thus not surprising that predicting whether a movie will 'flop' has developed into a 'profession' of its own and efforts at making correct predictions are becoming increasingly more sophisticated. In 2013 Google published a report claiming it could calculate the success of a movie with 94 per cent accuracy on the basis of searches for movie trailers (Google, 2013). Yet, it is questionable whether the drive for profits and the increasingly sophisticated attempts at predicting success lead to more diverse media contents.

Economists characterize media industries as economies of scale, these 'exist in any industry where marginal costs are lower than average costs. When the cost of providing an extra unit of a good falls as the scale of output expands, then economies of scale are present' (Doyle, 2005, p. 13). For example, the fixed costs of making a television programme are high but the cost of distributing that programme to an extra consumer is nil or very low. This makes it hard for new firms to enter the market. Arguably, new media technologies offer opportunities for lowering some costs, but at the same time they create what economists term 'economies of scope'. These 'arise when there are some shared overheads or other efficiency gains available that make it more cost-effective for two or more related products to be produced and sold jointly, rather than separately. Savings may arise if specialist inputs gathered for one product can be re-used in another' (ibid., p. 14). An example in this respect is a single news organization that supplies contents to its print, broadcast and online media, which leads to significant savings. Cost-effectiveness can lead to the repurposing of contents, and that not only between different media platforms (see for example Erdal, 2009) but also between different sectors of the media industries (see Chris, 2006 on the repurposing across broadcast and cable channels).

We should, however, not overestimate the extent of changes facilitated by the emergence and spread of new media technologies (see for example Fenton, 2010, particularly Chapter 3; Mansell, 2004). Arguments about the disruptive nature of new media technologies, such as their ability to demolish the monopolies existing in 'old media' has been questioned (see for example Winseck, 2002; Latzer, 2009). Also, in broadcasting it has become clear that economies of scale and scope continue to exist despite the emergence of new companies, particularly in the market with on-demand video contents. Players on the video-on-demand market such as Netflix, Amazon Prime, Now TV or Hulu receive a lot of attention, not only in relation to their annual financial reports but also in terms of the artistic quality of their outputs. (For example, original Netflix series such as *House of Cards* and *Orange is the New Black* have received significant critical acclaim, and in July 2014 Netflix collected a total of 31 Emmy nominations.) There is no question that consumers have embraced on-demand contents and incorporated them into their lifestyles but so far the change has not been as significant as some expected. For example, in the UK in 2013–14 the average time spent watching live TV per day declined by 11 minutes (to 193.3 minutes). Some of this is due to an increase (on average by 1 minute a day) in time-shifted TV viewing (viewing of programmes recorded and subsequently played back on a television set within seven days of live broadcast, as well as viewing after pausing or rewinding live TV) but the change is largely due to the watching of on-demand content (Ofcom, 2015).

Yet, questions about the future growth of companies such as Netflix are raised on a regular basis because they do not have control over internet access and the speed of streaming. In the words of a *Washington Post* writer: 'The world of television is dominated by big, entrenched players: broadcasters such as ABC and CBS, and cable companies such as Comcast that run the piping of the Internet and hope to get even bigger' (Kang, 2014). Cecilia Kang goes on to argue that Netflix's fight with cable providers is a challenge for government regulators and its survival depends on how audiences will behave in the future: 'Do they continue to pay Comcast for a big package of channels? Or do they abandon the bundle and subscribe to a mix of streaming video services such as Netflix and Amazon Prime, streamed through their Apple TV or Google's Android TV.' Some barriers to entry that exist in television broadcasting – namely government policy (through the granting of licences); the presence of dominant existing broadcasters; availability of suitable programming ('access to and reasonable prices for desirable programming in film and program libraries and to studios, directors, writers, actors, and technical personnel needed to produce attractive programming are necessary for successful entry' (Picard and Chon, 2004, p. 170)); audience behaviour and 'the necessity for entrants to overcome long-established uses of television and set patterns of viewing and channel choice' (ibid., p. 170) – also apply to video-on-demand producers.

Apart from other players who provide video-on-demand content only, Netflix's competitors include HBO Now, seen by some as the most 'threatening' because as a content company it has a large range of suitable programming available (see for example Learmonth, 2015), and this links to the second barrier that Picard and Chon identified. They argue that:

> Government policies can help reduce barriers as a means of increasing competition and the number of firms in an industry. ... One mechanism is guaranteed and subsidized loan funds that provide venture capital or capital for technology acquisition. Operation subsidies that provide another source of revenue and reduce operating losses in start-up firms can also be provided in some settings. Preferential awarding of licenses and franchises so that small companies have advantages in entering broadcasting or telecommunications is another mechanism of overcoming barriers for new firms.
>
> (ibid., p. 171)

They, however, conclude that '[c]ompetition policy alone does not guarantee achievement of the basic social objectives for the broadcasting industry such as maintaining a pluralism of views or providing greater variety in programs. Because competition alone does not ensure plurality or diversity of programming, merely lowering barriers to entry in the broadcasting market will not produce optimal outcomes' (ibid., p. 174).

It is clear from the discussion thus far that regulatory interventions may be needed in order to enable a diversity of media players to enter a market, but competition as such may be particularly unsuitable for achieving social objectives associated with media. However, we can assume that if media industries compete fairly, they will provide economic benefits for consumers as well as for society at large. Also, as already mentioned, media are prone to market failure and concerns about the consequences of concentration should be discussed at least briefly here. Media are especially prone to concentration – an increased presence of one (monopoly) or a few companies (oligopoly) in a market – which is undesirable for a number of reasons. From an economic policy perspective it is important to maintain fair competition because it benefits a variety of stakeholders. The European Commission provides the following reasoning:

Low prices for all: the simplest way for a company to gain a high market share is to offer a better price. ... Not only is this good for consumers – when more people can afford to buy products, it encourages businesses to produce and boosts the economy in general.

Better quality: Competition also encourages businesses to improve the quality of goods and services they sell – to attract more customers and expand market share. ...

More choice: In a competitive market, businesses will try to make their products different from the rest. ...

Innovation: To deliver this choice, and produce better products, businesses need to be innovative. ...

Better competitors in global markets: Competition within the EU helps make European companies stronger outside the EU too.

(Europa, 2015)

Importantly, there are also factors other than economic issues at stake when we consider media concentration. James Curran summarizes these:

The first is that private concentration of symbolic power potentially distorts the democratic process. ... The second ... is that the power potentially at the disposal of media moguls tends to be exerted in a one-sided way. ... The third ... is that the concentration of market power can stifle competition.

(Curran, 2002)

He goes on to argue that a fourth concern can be added to this list:

The dominant position ... – that media concentration undoubtedly exists but matters relatively little – fairly accurately reflects the balance of opinion, both in the relevant academic literature and in wider political debate. This is giving rise to a one-sided protection of our freedoms: a state of constant alert against the abuse of state power over the media, reflected in the development of numerous safeguards, not matched by an equivalent vigilance and set of safeguards directed against the abuse of shareholder power over the media.

(ibid.)

The fact that concentration raises issues other than economic ones and that tackling it requires strategies other than competition policy interventions is echoed by Meier and Trappel:

Some national and international organizations refer to media concentration only and entirely under aspects of competition law. Within this concept, all measures in respect of media concentration are analysed from the point of view of possible distortion of competition law. ... [In contrast,] the public policy concept of media concentration research aims at describing potential effects on the public interest, rather than on competition. Both concepts, however, are interrelated to some degree.

(1998, p. 40)

The limitations of advertising as a funding model

We can see from the above that media have special economic characteristics and (imperfect) competition does not necessarily ensure a diversity of media players in a market, a situation that is unlikely to change as a consequence of the possibilities offered by new media technologies. In this section I explore issues related to advertising, a key source of income for media companies. It has been suggested that advertising, which plays a central role in market competition, reduces the supply of minority interest programmes and tends to shut off non-commercial opinions and non-market forms of life (Keane, 1991). Media most often operate on a dual product market because they generate contents (of various types – films, video games, music and so on) and at the same time they also produce an audience that can be sold to advertisers (see for example Picard, 1989; McManus, 1992). It is important to note here that '[a]dvertising is a faulty funding mechanism in that it creates an incentive for the broadcaster to maximize not overall viewer welfare but the supply of whatever mix of programming yields the audience volumes, while patterns of intensity of viewer demand for different sorts of output may be ignored' (Doyle, 2002, p. 67; see also Metykova, 2013). It may seem that advertising as a means of driving consumer behaviour has been with us for ever. (On other roles of advertising, particularly as a cultural product see Lears, 1994; Davis, 2013; Wharton, 2013.) However, its biggest growth can be traced to the United States in the 19th century and historical explorations suggest that it was actually severely resisted (Vos and Li, 2013).

Advertisers are interested in buying particular audiences and require data not only about the size of an audience but also about its composition and consumption habits. Advertising and marketing agencies have used a range of methods for measuring audiences – including diaries, audimeters (for radio and television), people meters (developed for television), surveys, focus groups, interviews. Indeed, some of these audience measurement methods were developed by advertising/marketing companies, including the national people meter by Nielsen Holdings N.V. (see Nielsen, 2015). Companies are constantly seeking improved methods for measuring audiences, particularly online. In 2014, the UK's national newspaper industry started a review of its metrics for tracking readership across various digital platforms (Haggerty, 2014), while the Interactive Advertising Bureau – comprising more than 600 companies that sell 86 per cent of online advertising in the United States – had already prepared guidelines for measuring audience reach related to internet-based content and advertising (iab, 2015).

Advertising reduces the supply of minority interest programmes; in other words, if an audience is not sizeable enough to be sold to an advertiser, it is unlikely to have media contents produced for it. Thus although the role of ethnic minority media in maintaining the identities, cultures and political engagement of ethnic minority populations (see for example Cottle, 2000; Lind, 2003; Geissler and Potker, 2008) has been well documented, in their case advertising as a funding model fails due to small audience size (for example Browne, 2005). Even if a minority audience is sizeable enough, it may not be the most desirable one for advertisers because it may be an audience with lower incomes, which tends to be the case of minorities: in the US 'the wealth of white households was 13 times the median wealth of black households in 2013' (Kochhar and Fry, 2014). For this reason there will not be sufficient programming available for them, as Brown and Cavazos (2002) demonstrated in the case of African Americans and US programming in the late 1990s. Since then audiences have become more fragmented and content makers as well as advertisers target ever more precisely (demographically) defined audiences so we could expect that minority audiences will be able to choose from a greater diversity of contents. This, however, does not seem to be the case: for example, John Sinclair (2009) found that despite the increased movement of people across borders, they are largely ignored by mainstream corporate advertisers who dominate the media market in their destination country. The industry-led discussion on this topic began only in the 2010s: for example, in June 2014 Nielsen, the global information and measurement company, published a report on the bilingual brain as a step towards understanding the consumption habits of Hispanic Millennials on the ground that Hispanics and Millennials comprised 'two of the fastest growing and increasingly important consumer groups in the U.S.' (Nielsen, 2014).

The quality of journalism that is funded from advertising income has also been questioned. Some argue that the pressures on media to make ever bigger profits result in a shift to market journalism. 'Advertisers do not pay for high-level quality journalism, but for the requested "quality" of the sector of society to be reached. Market journalism, however, provides for a different construction of reality in the media and for a substantially different media reality. Its first and foremost objective is not to inform but to satisfy the targeted sector of society' (Meier and Trappel, 1998, p. 57). Chapter 2 discussed the importance of diverse credible information for maintaining deliberations about issues that are of concern to citizens rather than consumers. Financial pressures became more acute in the aftermath of the financial crash of 2002 (and the financial crisis of 2008) when media companies suffered significant losses of advertising revenue combined with increased competition for advertising from online players. (See for example Berte and De Bens, 2008 on advertising challenges and opportunities in the online environment; Mitchell and Matsa, 2015 on the declining value of US newspapers since 1993.) This impact has been well documented in the case of news production: see, for example, in relation to the steady decline of local news, Fenton et al., 2010; foreign news, Kumar, 2011; Otto and Meyer, 2012; and investigative journalism, House of Lords, 2012; cf. Feldstein, 2006.

The decline in the advertising revenue of print media was combined with a lack of successful business models for their online operations. Major well-established newspapers attempted to develop new ways of generating revenue in the online environment, with *The New York Times* – heralded for the quality of its journalism – leading the way. In March 2011 the newspaper introduced a metered paywall and its performance has been closely watched by industry specialists, stock holders as well as academics. (See Myllylahti (2014) for an analysis of the paywall models adopted in eight countries.) After fluctuations in income, the company had some good news in 2014: a 2.6 per cent rise in total revenue for the first three months of the year and an increase in both print and online advertising revenue for the first time in several years (Somaiya, 2014). It is, however, clear that the business model was not yet consolidated because the paper's leaked digital strategy (*The New York Times*, 2014) outlined further actions. Indeed, Clay Shirky from New York University responded to Margaret Sullivan's (*The New York Times'* public editor) statement that 70 per cent of the newspaper's total revenue still coming from print was a sign of the robustness of the business model with a somewhat stark prediction about the sustainability of the newspaper's print version:

> The problem with print is that the advantageous returns to scale from physical distribution of newspapers become disadvantageous when scale shrinks. The ad revenue from a print run of 500,000 would be 16 percent less than for 600,000 at best, but the costs wouldn't fall by anything like 16%, eroding print margins. There is some threshold, well above 100,000 copies and probably closer to 250,000, where nightly print runs stop making economic sense. ... When no advertiser can reach a million readers in any print ad in the Times (2017, on present evidence) and weekday advertising reaches less than half a million (2018, using the 6 percent decline figure you quoted), there will be downward pressure on C.P.M.s [cost per thousand, the cost to the advertiser per thousand readers]. This makes no sense, of course, since pricing ads per thousand should make advertisers indifferent to overall circulation, but marketing departments have never been run terribly logically. So it seems likely to me that after the early, rapid decline, we are now in a period of shallow, secular decay, which will give way to a late-stage period of rapid decline.
>
> (Sullivan, 2015)

Alternatives to advertising?

It is thus clear that advertising as a funding mechanism has its shortcomings when it comes to financing contents for minority audiences, and also in relation to quality journalism and contents that are socially desirable but may not attract a sufficiently large audience to be commercially viable. This section considers two instances in which market competition has failed to create sustainable media platforms – the cases of minorities and local communities. Even though there are other funding options available (for example direct payment from viewers), these are unlikely to alleviate market failure. This is explained by the economic theory of discrimination: small groups with atypical preferences will not be served by the market because of impersonal economic processes – simply because they are too small to generate a profit (Cooper, 2003). While advertising as a source of income is important for minority media, the wide range of ways in which they are funded – government subsidies, foundation grants, sponsorship, licence fees (mostly applicable to minority media run as part of the public service broadcasting system), institutional support (for example from churches), voluntary donations, sale of media services and products and reliance on volunteers which saves running costs and/or salaries – suggests that advertising revenues are not sufficient to maintain them. Browne makes an important observation in this respect: 'Financing takes a host of shapes, in ethnic as well as in mainstream media. The most important difference is that ethnic minority services are more likely to be on thin edge than are mainstream media' (2005, p.105). As already suggested, there are two important factors that explain why minority media tend to be of little interest to advertisers: their audiences are small in size and they also tend to involve low income groups.

Local news plays an important role in the lives of their audiences. It is key to local democratic processes but local newspapers, radio stations and television channels have been 'in a crisis' as a result of a combination of factors, including declining audiences and advertising revenue as well as the migration of news online (see for example Franklin and Murphy, 1998; Barnett, 2010, cf. Mitchell et al., 2015 on local news in three US cities). In the UK policy makers decided to resolve this crisis by the introduction of local television licences when the first stations launched in 2013. This policy move was widely criticized during its preparation (see for example Fenton et al., 2010) and its success was questioned within a few years of implementation as some of the local television stations went bankrupt, cut staff or reduced the amount of local output. For example, in August 2014 London's local television station London Live announced that it would cease producing original entertainment programmes (which amounted to 2.5 hours daily) and would broadcast the 8 hours of fresh daily content required by its licence in the form of news and current affairs (Sweney, 2014).

New media technologies have emerged as providers of local news (which is difficult to provide on a commercial basis) with the mushrooming of a variety of websites with local and hyperlocal contents. These news websites vary greatly in their scope and audience reach (for an overview of the British case, see Williams et al., 2014). However, importantly, producers of local and hyperlocal sites tend to see their activity as a form of active community participation and most of them are 'not motivated by economic gain, [although] the overall lack of revenues being generated could threaten the longer term sustainability of hyperlocal publishing' (ibid., p. 5). Yet, '[d]espite lacking institutional and professional support, a significant minority have also carried out local watchdog investigative journalism' (ibid., p. 4). Problems with the long-term sustainability of non-profit local news have also been widely studied in the United States. A 2015 report by the Knight Foundation – that has invested in many US non-profit news organizations – concluded that: 'The field of nonprofit news, as illustrated by the 20 organizations profiled in [the] study, has continued to scale its impact and inch closer toward more sustainable business models. But progress has been uneven and for the majority of organizations in the study, sustainability is just a premise on the distant horizon' (Knight Foundation, 2015; cf. Konieczna and Robinson, 2014 who also acknowledge the problematic sustainability of non-profit news organizations).

In the United States 'minority ownership enhancements were in keeping with policies adopted by the FCC to promote diversity on the airwaves. Diversity, along with competition and localism, constituted the core of how the FCC defined the "public interest" obligations of broadcasters, and since the 1940s the Commission had imposed ownership restrictions on licensees to promote diversity' (Perlman, 2012, p. 361). As already suggested, the FCC's stance changed in the 1980s, the repeal of the Fairness Doctrine was an indication of this change and the FCC's Financial Interest and Syndication Rules that prevented broadcast networks from owning the programming that appeared on air were also relaxed (and repealed in the early 1990s, see for example Einstein, 2004). Perlman argues that more recent initiatives undertaken by the FCC to promote diversity have been cautious.

[In 2008 the Commission] adopted a 'Diversity Order' to benefit 'eligible entities', defined as small businesses: radio stations with no more than $6.5 million in annual earnings, television stations with no more than $13 million. The FCC did not adopt a definition of 'eligible entity' that privileged broadcast owners who are people of colour or women. ... In addition, the Commission has sought comments on whether, in the future, it would be advisable and constitutionally sound to revise its definition of 'eligible entity' that would include specifically race- and gender-based categories. Such timidity in approach arguably stems from three decades of court decisions rendering racial classifications constitutionally suspect, especially in the realm of broadcasting policy.

(Perlman, 2012, p. 366)

This highlights the political nature of policy making as discussed in Chapter 1 and emphasizes the influence of the political and judicial arenas in decision making about normative issues related to the media.

The larger framework of deregulation and privatization

In the United States the term 'deregulation' has been used to describe the shift in the government's regulatory framework that evolved in the 1980s. A relevant example for my argument here involves the telecommunications industry which 'began life as a highly regulated monopoly in private hands' with 'the setting of rates and operating criteria by the government as a means of safeguarding the public interest' (Philip and Tsoi, 1988, p. 259). The deregulation of the telecommunications industry was to lead to greater competition (the AT&T monopoly was identified as a particular problem in the 1970s) that would mainly benefit consumers (that is, reduce prices) and businesses. However, writing in 1988, George Philip and Shao Hing Tsoi argued that 'so far only the business sector has benefitted from competition' and that applied not only to companies operating in the telecommunications market but also the marketing and advertising industries. Yet, 'balanced against the benefits are the grievances about deregulation. They are mainly from two sources: ordinary people who see the deterioration of public utilities, and the small telecommunications firms who, despite the promise of a golden future, are still finding it hard to compete effectively with AT&T' (ibid., pp. 262–3). The Fairness Doctrine was suspended in 1987 and an important factor in the decision were 'interpretations of this [First] amendment favouring the rights of broadcasting *corporations*, and not only individuals to enjoy freedom of speech' (Harvey, 1998, p. 542, original emphasis). Harvey goes on to argue that the 'view of broadcasting as an "instrument" of democracy was one which – while it remained current in certain intellectual quarters – was largely rejected in American government thinking and in regulatory practice by the 1980s' (ibid., p. 545).

In Western European countries the policy changes of the 1980s can be described as privatization – the transfer of public assets or function to the private sector – accompanied with the creation of new regulatory bodies and the widening of the scope of agencies promoting competition.

> in Europe the terms 'deregulation' and 'privatization' gained sudden currency – even in Britain the words were scarcely heard before 1979 – without a clear understanding of regulation as a distinct mode of policy-making. In fact, regulation became a topic of scholarly and political interest only in the wake of the deregulation and privatization debate.
>
> (Majone, 1994, p. 55)

European governments differed in their enthusiasm for privatization in the field of media. Kenneth Dyson and Peter Humphreys (1986) point out that '[I]n some Western European countries, such as Britain, these pressures met with the ready compliance, even encouragement, of governments; in others, such as France, they asserted themselves regardless of government policy and established practices' (pp. 99–100). The role of the US in setting the trend towards privatization and deregulation is emphasized by Calabrese, for example. 'Of course, there is a vitally important global dimension to all of this, in that for many years the US has served as both the model and, when models fail, the primary source of political and economic pressure, to get the rest of the world to fall into line with its media policy frameworks' (2004, p.112). The literature on policy developments refers to both deregulation and privatization. However, Murdock points out that deregulation is a misnomer.

> What is at stake is not so much the number of rules but the shift in their overall rationale, away from a defence of the public interest (however that was conceived) and towards the promotion of corporate interests. Communications corporations benefit from this shift at two levels. They not only gain from changes to the general laws governing corporate activity in areas such as trade-union rights but, more importantly, they have also gained considerably from the relaxation of the additional rules designed to prevent undue concentration in the market-place of ideas and to ensure diversity of expression.
>
> (1997, pp. 12–13)

Attention has been drawn to another characteristic of the shift in governments' approach to regulation: the prevalence of regulation after the event rather than pro-active regulation. In Feintuck's words the reactive shift results in 'accepting and legitimising market trends rather than establishing positive targets for regulation' (1999, p. 164).

In the 1990s and 2000s a number of academics (see for example Murdock, 1992; Bagdikian, 1997; McKenna, 2000; McChesney, 2004) explored the expanding shift from citizen-oriented to consumer-oriented regulation. In the US the impact was particularly strong in radio:

> [following the introduction of the 1996 Telecommunications Act] well over half of US stations have been sold, and a stunning consolidation has hit the industry. One firm, Clear Channel, now owns nearly 1200 stations. Every market is dominated by two to three firms that own nearly all the stations between them.
>
> (McChesney, 2003, p. 129)

Much discussion followed the case of the 2002 Minot train derailment in which hazardous materials were released into the atmosphere when local radio stations owned by Clear Channel failed to alert the public to the emergency, arguably because the stations were left unmanned (see Klinenberg, 2008). The FCC's investigation into the role of deregulation in disaster reporting found a number of failures in the use of the Emergency Alert System (FCC, 2015). Although the US media market has evolved somewhat since the first half of the 2000s, a handful of media corporations continue to dominate. In his 2004 book *The New Media Monopoly* Ben Bagdikian highlighted five such corporations – News Corp, Viacom, Bertelsman, GE and Disney.

In the first half of 2015, a case from the US highlighted public concerns about the potentially detrimental impact of mergers (ownership consolidation) on competition (and as a consequence on benefits to consumers) and also on the quality of democratic debate. The potential merger between Time Warner and Comcast which was to be approved by the FCC prompted widespread opposition from grassroots organizations that used new media technologies in their campaigns to mobilize opposition to the proposed deal for very clear reasons. In the words of the campaign organization Free Press:

> Comcast is the country's #1 cable and Internet company and Time Warner Cable is #2. Put them together and you get a single giant controlling a massive share of our nation's TV and Internet-access

markets. Putting this much power in the hands of one company is dangerous. This deal would lead to less consumer choice, less diversity and higher cable bills.

(Free Press, 2015)

In the end, Comcast withdrew its bid of $45 billion, following serious concerns expressed by staff at the FCC about the merger risks outweighing the benefits to the public interest. The move was welcomed by the chairman of the FCC Tom Wheeler:

Comcast and Time Warner Cable's decision to end Comcast's proposed acquisition of Time Warner Cable is in the best interests of consumers. The proposed transaction would have created a company with the most broadband and video subscribers in the nation alongside the ownership of significant programming interests. Today, an online video market is emerging that offers new business models and greater consumer choice. The proposed merger would have posed an unacceptable risk to competition and innovation especially given the growing importance of high-speed broadband to online video and innovative new services. I am proud of our close working relationship throughout the review process with the Antitrust Division of the Department of Justice. Our collaboration provided both agencies with a deeper understanding of the important issues of innovation and competition that the proposed transaction raised.

(FCC, 2015a)

Conclusion

This chapter has discussed some economic characteristics of media organizations and their outputs that differentiate them from other consumer goods. It has used the metaphor of the marketplace of ideas to illustrate the rationales underlying media regulation, a marketplace that relies on competition as a way of ensuring not only economic but also socially desirable outcomes. This approach to regulating the media is different from those outlined in Chapter 2 in that it focusses mainly on ensuring a diversity of players in a market. It has become clear in the course of the chapter that competition-based regulation of the media industries has shortcomings when ensuring media's social and cultural roles. The basic premise of competition regulation – within an economic as opposed to a public interest framework – is that if media organizations compete fairly, they will provide (economic) benefits for consumers as well as for the wider society. However, it needs to be remembered that perfect competition is almost non-existent and that regulatory interventions are necessary to tackle market failure. We saw in Chapter 2 that, in order to ensure socially desirable outcomes associated with media, regulatory and policy interventions are necessary. Similarly, regulatory interventions are necessary in order to ensure fair competition or prevent anti-competitive behaviour. However, we need to keep in mind that competition does not necessarily result in social and cultural benefits associated with media. The chapter considered barriers that prevent the entry of new players in a market (and hence hinder the existence of a diversity of competitors) and it argued that the emergence of new media technologies does not remove them. The role of advertising – as a key source of funding – has been discussed in relation to the marginalization of the interests and voices of groups that are not sizeable or attractive enough for advertisers. The final section of the chapter considered the larger framework of changing regulatory practices and rationales and their consequences.

4 Transnationalization of Media and Audiences

Previous chapters have suggested that contemporary societies and their media systems face challenges that are linked to the transnational movement of people as well as media products. Audiences – that may have been previously understood as homogeneous – have become more fragmented (or diversified) and their needs and interests are not necessarily readily served by national media. The role of media in fostering a national culture and a national public sphere has been discussed in Chapter 2 and it is important to remind ourselves here that the degree of the public sphere's openness to maintenance of difference is crucial for inclusion. Developments relating to the transnational movements of people and products and of audience fragmentation pose particular challenges in terms of the democratic roles of media; in other words the key issue is how we can ensure that the mediated public sphere is truly inclusive and diverse. Technological advances have enabled a greater availability of media contents from all around the world and media consumption habits – as already suggested in Chapter 1 – have been viewed by some as indicators of the unwillingness of migrant groups to integrate into their new societies. New media technologies have contributed to easier access to media contents and provide a cheap and ready-made way in which migrants can maintain their links with their countries of origin. In this chapter we turn our attention to the transnationalization of media audiences, an increasingly widespread phenomenon due to growing migration, the establishment of large migrant communities and easy access to transnational media.

The first part of this chapter considers the transnationalization of media, a relatively recent phenomenon that can be distinguished from globalization. One aspect of the globalization of communication involved the creation of broadcasters with a global reach, evidenced by the expansion of US cable networks into global markets in the 1980s, and resulted in (uneven) flows of media contents. Importantly, in some cases the creation of transnational broadcasters was led by political and social considerations and this chapter outlines the efforts of the EU in using media for the creation of a pan-European identity. The strategies of European leaders were also guided by concerns about the domination of US programmes on European television screens. In the 1970s and 1980s discussions about the dominance of Western media players on the global scene unfolded under the auspices of the United Nations Educational, Scientific and Cultural Organization (UNESCO), but it took until the early 2000s for a new global player – the Qatari-based and sponsored Al Jazeera – to emerge as a global news organization providing alternative news that challenges Western ideologies, an issue discussed by scholars as well as politicians.

The chapter then moves on to discuss the significance of the accessibility of transnational media contents for migrant communities, a particularly important issue since the late 1980s when satellite broadcasting became available. The consumption of contents from migrants' countries of origin has been represented as a threat to national culture and unity in some public discourses (which tend to regard national identity as a zero-sum game), and the chapter suggests that it is a much more complex phenomenon so that conceptualizations that work with the national frame have serious limitations. Methodological nationalism has characterized empirical studies on news and television flows and the taken-for-granted framework of the nation-state also characterizes some research on diasporas and media. The final section of the chapter explores aspects of new media technologies in relation to the transnationalization of media contents and also refers to a selection of recent directions of research on the use of new media technologies by migrants and minorities.

The making of European television

The availability and abundance of international media contents for those of us living in the developed world may seem to be a recent phenomenon. However, the evolution of international communication channels has been ongoing since the mid-19th century. Chalaby (2005) argues that the current transnationalization of media – when international media spaces and flows are no longer the sole preserve of Western-based conglomerates – can be understood as the third phase in the evolution of international communication. In the first phase – internationalization – the development of the telegraph led to the establishment of the first corporations with an international scope (for

more on the main players and particularly the global character of the
media system post-1860s, see Winseck and Pike, 2009) and the first
international media markets (and indeed news agencies, see for example Boyd-Barrett, 1980). In the second phase – globalization – 'a new
paradigm began to emerge in the 1960s, when a series of innovations in
the field of telecommunications – prompted by advances in computing,
microelectronics and space-related technologies – provoked a second
explosion in international communication' (ibid., p. 29). In this period
television stations began broadcasting across borders and Marshall
McLuhan (1962) famously declared that we all lived in a 'global vil-
lage'. In the 1980s US cable networks became important global players
with The Cable News Network (CNN) emerging as the first global channel in the world, gradually expanding its coverage and launching CNN
International Europe/Middle East/Africa in 1985, CNN International
Asia Pacific in 1989 and CNN International North America in 2000.
Other US cable networks also expanded to Europe and beyond; for
example, Music Television (MTV) Europe launched in 1987. Scholars,
policy makers and activists have expressed concerns about the global
one-way flow of news, music and consumer culture that characterized
the expansion of these cable networks (see for example Banks, 1997;
Herman and McChesney, 1997; Juluri, 2002) and could potentially lead
to the development of a homogeneous global culture. Some of the key
developments in the debates about the dominance of Western companies on global media markets are discussed below.

The establishment of media players whose activities crossed borders
was, however, not always motivated merely by profit, and the efforts
made by European countries to establish pan-European television
broadcasting as a way of fostering a European identity exemplify a
number of interesting points. The predecessor of the European Union –
the European Economic Community – was created by the Treaty of
Rome in 1957 (with Belgium, France, Germany, Italy, Luxembourg and
the Netherlands as the original signatories). However, efforts at creating pan-European broadcasting predate it: the European Broadcasting
Union (EBU) – originally a union of 23 public service broadcasters – was
founded in 1950. EBU's achievements evolved gradually and, while
some advocated the creation of a truly European public sphere (which
has not materialized yet (2016) – see Brüggemann and Schulz-Forberg,
2009; Metykova and Preston, 2009), it is the Eurovision Song Contest
that has become its most recognized and popular achievement. As
Bourdon points out, it was actually launched 'mostly with the intention of popularizing the EBU, an institution the audience knew little

about. The operation was successful but the patient died: the Song Contest fast became highly popular, to the point that in many countries the word "Eurovision" refers not to a brave effort to broadcast in a truly European way, but to a specific event, the Song Contest itself' (2007, p. 265). However, the EBU was most active in news, with a variety of plans discussed from its very inception – a pan-European news channel or a European news agency – but in the end the organization set up a news exchange in 1959. In the early 1980s pan-European television was foregrounded by European Commission policy makers as an agent of European consciousness building (Bourdon, 2007; Polonska-Kimunguyi and Kimunguyi, 2011). However, the first pan-European channel launched by 16 EBU members and Rupert Murdoch's News International in 1989 was Eurosport, and although the idea of a pan-European news channel was first conceived in the early 1950s, it took until January 1993 to launch the Euronews channel.

Machill argues that European policy makers' assumptions about the significant role of a pan-European television channel in fostering European integration have been unfounded. 'The thought that a European television channel could have a similarly unifying effect in the heads of Europeans as the national TV stations have with regard to the citizens of individual nations has proven to be an inadmissible extension of precisely this *national* experience. In contrast to a nation, Europe is not unified politico-culturally' (1998, p. 429, original emphasis). Bourdon argues in a similar vein and points out that the failures surrounding the creation of a pan-European television channel resulted from European leaders' outdated understanding of television as an all-powerful medium (the so-called hypodermic needle theory of the 1930s and 1940s which has since been discredited and considered simplistic) combined with 'a dated, but still very powerful, communicative and culture-based view of the nation' (Bourdon, 2007, p. 275). He goes on to argue that:

> If television can play a part in the construction of Europe, it is not by artificially putting together a 'European programme', not to mention a 'European channel', but by reporting Europe more, and in a more open and democratic way (not simply as a topic of bickering between countries and inside individual countries) – by developing its 'European beat'. But then, European institutions would also have to be newsworthy enough – and care less about direct communication policy than about public relations.
>
> (ibid., p. 278)

David Morley and Kevin Robins argue that the approach adopted by policy makers (and also by some scholars) works with some problematic assumptions: 'The power of the media is assumed and never demonstrated. Such an assumption is grounded in the model of the communication process [within which] communications technologies are the active and determining forces, whilst culture and identity are passive and reactive' (1995, p. 71). They go on to argue that:

> If we are really to understand the relation between communication, culture and identity, then we must move beyond this deterministic model of the communication process. Within this prevailing framework, cultural identities can only ever be responsive and reactive to the controlling stimulus of communications technologies. What is needed is a better formulation of the problem, one that takes cultural identity as a problematical and a central category.
>
> (ibid., p. 71)

The establishment of the Euronews channel has also been identified as a defensive move, an attempt to protect against the dominance of CNN in particular and US television programmes in general. 'By the 1960s, the USA completely dominated international flows of television programming and television became closely linked to concerns about American popular culture more generally. ... Ironically, in the 1970s and early 1980s, when the cultural imperialism thesis was at its peak, US television's international domination was in decline' (Hesmondhalgh, 2013, p. 278). Yet, concerns about the competitiveness of the European media industries when faced with US competitors who were dominant global players were on the radar of the European Commission in that period. In a study that mapped trends in international television flows between 1973 and 1983, Tapio Varis argues that 'US producers and companies are the largest program exporters in the world; and, in relation to total output, US television networks import fewer foreign programs than any other country and one might claim that foreign programs are not shown at all in the United States' (1986, p. 237). Research conducted in the 1970s and 1980s reveals the domination of US fiction on European television, prompting the use of the term 'Dallasification of television content' (see for example De Bens and de Smaele, 2001). Referring to the same period:

> Discussions of 'Americanization', whether among diplomats, media industry officials, or intellectuals, are part of a more far-reaching

discussion about the impact of modernity, the massification of cultural forms, and the economies of scale whereby market expansion involved not only Europe but also the rest of the world. ... In Europe the debate is particularly poignant because in previous centuries what could retrospectively be called 'European culture' had dominated world markets and elite tastes through colonial ties. In more contemporary discourses about European identity, Americanization has been defined as the 'other' against which Europe must defend itself – even as American popular culture was said, perhaps only part in jest, to be the only culture that all Europeans shared, or at the very least Europeans' 'second culture'.

(Siefert, 2007, p. 165)

Morley and Robins (1995) point out that for European leaders the key questions were: 'Where will these pictures come from? Who will capture the market – and the employment – for producing and transmitting them?' and argue that: 'If US dominance is to be challenged ... then the construction of a pan-European industry and market is imperative' (pp. 34–5).

The European-level response to this challenge came in the form of the Directive 89/552/EEC 'Television without Frontiers' of 3 October 1989 that created a European common market in television broadcasts and programme supply. The Directive also aimed to promote independent production and distribution enterprises and established a European content quota (see for example Collins, 1994). However, the global dominance of certain players and the one-way flow of news and other media contents (from the West to the rest of the world) represented a much larger and long-existing issue.

One-way flow of media contents

The dominance of Western countries, particularly the United States, has characterized the news industries from early on. A 1953 study by UNESCO argues that six telegraphic agencies can be classified as world agencies (and these came into being between 1835 and 1918 during the internationalization phase), of which three originated in the US, one in France, one in the UK and one in the USSR (UNESCO, 1953). In the 1970s five news agencies dominated globally: AFP (France); AP (US); Reuters (UK); TASS (USSR) and UPI (US) (International Commission for the Study of Communication Problems, undated). This is not to suggest that there were no other news agencies operating (or attempting to operate) on the global news market. Indeed, the Inter Press Service was established in Latin America in the 1960s and the Non-Aligned News Pool in the 1970s by Yugoslav and other news agencies (on the globalization of news agencies see Boyd-Barrett and Rantanen, 1999; for an overview of key developments and research traditions on international communication and globalization see Mohammadi, 1997). In the 1970s and 1980s the concept of cultural imperialism (Schiller, 1969) was used to describe the way in which the cultures of developing countries were affected by flows of cultural texts from the 'West'.

'The "cultural imperialism thesis" held that, as the age of direct political and economic domination by colonial powers drew to an end, a new, more indirect form of international domination was beginning' (Hesmondhalgh, 2013, p. 272). This cultural domination was characterized by the imposition of 'Western' cultural products on non-'Western' countries, threatening or outright destroying indigenous cultural practices and traditions and having a strong homogenizing effect. Cultural imperialism as a concept has been widely criticized and the term globalization has largely replaced it.

> Globalization was a term largely developed by social theorists (such as Giddens 1991; Robertson 1990) working in very different contexts from the international policy forums and activist circles where the cultural imperialism thesis initially became widespread. ... Globalisation was intended to capture the increasing interconnectedness of different parts of the world. Partly because it referred to a wide variety of economic, political and cultural practices, it spread quickly to become the most widely discussed social science concept of the 1990s, going beyond academia to reach many other circles.
>
> (Hesmondhalgh, 2013, p. 273)

The inequalities in the global news flow became part of UNESCO's discussions about the nature and roles of communications worldwide and gained prominence from the mid-1970s to the mid-1980s with the particular aim of addressing imbalances in media coverage and media influence, although it also considered issues related to technologies, protection of journalists and similar. In 1980 UNESCO published the MacBride report, the full title of which is worth mentioning here: *Communication and Society Today and Tomorrow, Many Voices, One World: Towards a New More Just and More Efficient World Information and Communication Order* (International Commission for the Study of Communication Problems, 1980). The report sparked a debate on the so-called New World Information and Communication Order (NWICO) but it was condemned by the US and UK as an attack on the freedom of press and both countries withdrew their membership of UNESCO in protest – the US in 1984 and the UK in 1985. (On the continued relevance of the MacBride Report see for example the special issue 'The MacBride Report – 25 Years Later' of *Javnost – The Public* (No author, 2005).) Apart from inequalities, concerns were also expressed about the small number of news agencies that dominated the global news market and had their spheres of influence, and were actually promoting national interests rather than competing in the production and sale of impartial news. Kruglak (1968) draws attention to the cartel agreement among the major news agencies that was reached in 1870 and which led to the division of the world into zones in which each of the news agencies had an exclusive right to gather and distribute news.

> Wolff was given control over the transmission of news to and from Germany, Austria, the Netherlands, Scandinavia, Russia, and the Balkans. ... Similarly, Havas was allocated Italy, Switzerland, Spain, Portugal, Central and South America, and Egypt (in association with Reuters). Reuters was given the Far East, the British Empire, Turkey, and Egypt (in association with Havas). The American news agency, the New York Associated Press, a junior member of the cartel, was given the territory of the United States.
>
> (p. 22)

Kruglak goes on to argue that during the First World War news agencies played a role in propaganda and it took until the appearance of a new player not bound by cartel agreements – United Press – and the 1930s that the grip of the dominant news agencies began to crumble. Writing in the 1960s, Kruglak suggests that by then there was more competition on the news market and thus at least in theory there should be a greater supply and diversity of international news. However, he points out the key role of the editor – the gatekeeper (see Chapter 5 for more on gatekeeping) – and argues that 'it will never be possible to eliminate national bias from the actions of the editor of a national news agency (or from the correspondent of an international news agency)' (ibid., p. 24). This conclusion leads him to a radical proposal: the establishment of a doctrine of fairness in international news. (As discussed in Chapter 3, the doctrine had already been introduced in the US in the 1940s with the aim of ensuring the coverage of controversial issues of public importance and for the presentation of contrasting views concerning such issues.) 'If International Agency A transmits its version of a fact and International Agency B's is different, the national news agency editor can look at the material with the fairness doctrine in mind and summarize both points of view. This may confuse some readers, but in the long run it will enable them to reach the first plateau of understanding in international affairs' (ibid., p. 24).

The globalizing phase is also characterized by the marketization of media industries (for more on marketization see Chapters 2 and 3). Developments in Western Europe in the 1980s and early 1990s echoed those in the United States. European public service broadcasters lost their monopoly and commercial players established themselves on media markets. Hesmondhalgh points out that, '[as] with the shift towards marketization in the USA, the pulling apart of the PSB system in liberal democracies was based on a struggle over how best to organise cultural production in an era when its perceived economic importance was on the rise' (2013, p. 140) This process also affected European countries that had a long tradition of government intervention in media, such as France. Marketization of media resulted in a greater number of players on the markets and a greater specialization of media. In an article on the fragmentation of French radio audiences, Hervé Glevarec and Michel Pinet point out the importance of government legislation in the segmentation of radio outlets by 'format and age [which] was formalized in France by the law of 1 August 2000, which established differing quotas for songs in French, thus modifying the earlier law of 1996 according to the proportion of "new talent" or "new productions" that stations choose to showcase' (2008, p. 215).

A transnational media order

As mentioned in the opening of this chapter, Chalaby argues that the current phase in the evolution of media systems can be characterized as transnationalization. 'A transnational media order is coming into being that is remapping media spaces and involving new media practices, flows and products. An international reach is no longer the preserve of Western-based conglomerates' (Chalaby, 2005, p. 30; see also Thussu, 2000; Chalaby, 2005a). The emergence of Al Jazeera is often cited in discussions on the contra-flow of news (see for example Painter, 2008; Figenschou, 2014). Al Jazeera started broadcasting in Arabic in November 1996 from Doha in Qatar. It is a government-funded TV station which expanded globally: Al Jazeera English launched in 2006 and reached more than 270 million households in 140 countries in 2015. There is a wide range of academic studies exploring Al Jazeera's role as an alternative news provider, with particular attention being paid to the coverage of news that is expected to be ideologically biased – such as the Israeli–Palestinian conflict. Analyzing the departure from war journalism in the coverage of the conflict by Al Jazeera, Press TV (representing an alternative news broadcaster), BBC and CNN International, Ozohu-Suleiman (2014) concludes that

> the 'alternative perspective' is an inappropriate paradigm for explain-
> ing the roles of emerging non-western media in the context of
> the Israeli–Palestinian peace process. This is because they do not
> represent the peace journalism alternative to the dominant war
> perspective on the conflict. Second, there is a general tendency for
> peace propaganda to evolve into political peace journalism, in which
> media from both perspectives might not be seen as overtly war-
> inclined but seeking to reproduce peace propaganda in the Israeli–
> Palestinian conflict within the framework of peace journalism.
>
> (pp. 100–1)

In March 2011 Hillary Clinton – then US Secretary of State – expressed the view that the US was losing the information war as new players on the global media market – including Al Jazeera – were taking a lead in shaping the public's opinions about the United States (see for example Warrick, 2011). Clinton proposed that Al Jazeera's appeal was due to its provision of 'real news' as opposed to the infotainment broadcast by US media. We should, however, bear in mind that since the First World War international broadcasting has been used as a tool of public diplomacy which can be defined as 'efforts by the government of one nation to influence the public or elite opinion in a second nation for the purpose of turning the foreign policy of the target nation to advantage' (Manheim as quoted in Samuel-Azran, 2013, p. 1293). Approached from this perspective, Clinton's view can also be interpreted as a concern that the United States was losing the mediated public diplomacy battle.

Al Jazeera's reputation for shaping the contra-flow of news is most likely to be due to the fact that 'judged by appearances alone, few media outlets in the global South demonstrate contra-flow in action as effectively as the Al-Jazeera satellite channel' (Sakr in Thussu, 2007, p. 104; see also Wojcieszak, 2007). Naomi Sakr argues that at the onset Al Jazeera – which broadcast in Arabic only – was not conceived primarily as a source of counter-hegemonic contra-flow and that its changes in self-image are linked to world politics and often-conflicting assessments of its performance.

> Well before it launched into broadcasting in English, the station was routinely credited by Western observers with having 'taken on the West', even though broadcasters in languages other than Arabic could never have competed for the same Arabic-speaking audience. The station's supposed challenge to Western media was magnified in these reports at the very time when its staff were being harassed, imprisoned and even killed and its access to sources and audiences was being blocked. In the Arab world, meanwhile, smear campaigns portrayed the station as a lackey of US neo-imperialism or a plaything of Qatar's ruler, whereas its actual achievement was to create an unprecedented space for pan-Arab public discussion. To the extent that these depictions misrepresented reality, they suggest that Al-Jazeera's original Arabic-language operation did pose a threat to hegemonic interests and was predictably subject to processes of neutralisation and exclusion.
>
> (ibid., p. 115)

A number of scholars highlight the importance of distinguishing between Al Jazeera's Arabic output and that on Al Jazeera English because some studies suggest differences in their broadcasting norms, with the Al Jazeera English channel and website adhering to the professional values and norms of the Anglo/US model of journalism more closely (for an overview see for example Samuel-Azran, 2013, p. 1297). Although 'public opinion surveys in the Arab world have repeatedly indicated that Al Jazeera has effectively branded itself as an independent and credible media source ... critics assert that Al Jazeera is a political instrument designed to increase Qatar's international influence' (ibid., p. 1297). Indeed, Samuel-Azran concludes his analysis of Al Jazeera's (both Arabic and English) coverage of the Qatari–Saudi conflict that lasted from 2002 to 2007 by arguing that 'Qatar effectively promotes its public diplomacy goals by operating Al Jazeera as a hybrid network [private broadcaster and state-sponsored tool of public diplomacy] whose independence is limited by the boundaries of Qatar's crucial interests' (ibid., p. 1307). Other international news broadcasters have aimed to emulate Al Jazeera's success in establishing a reputation as an independent news broadcaster, but they have instead been associated with state-sponsored propaganda, including CCTV (Chinese), RT (formerly Russia Today, Russian) and Press TV (Iranian). In her analysis of the coverage of the global financial crisis of 2008 by Al Jazeera (AJE), CNN, RT and BBC World, Alexa Robertson argues for a more nuanced understanding of the ways in which global news media cover global crises (and events in more general).

> It can be argued that some channels (AJE, for example) are 'more global' than others when their framing strategies are considered. Nor should all global channels be relegated to the same corner of the newsroom – especially not the 'counter-hegemonics'. Where RT reports differently from BBC World and CNN in an 'old-fashioned' way (i.e. a way familiar from news reporting in the cold-war decades of the 1970s and 1980s, its world marked by great power rivalry), AJE reports differently, in a 'new-world-order' sort of way. Its world is also bigger and its component parts more interconnected. Whether or not it is a brave new world is a question that requires more empirical analysis.
>
> (Robertson, 2014, p. 623–4)

Although the literature on flows and contra-flows is varied and its use in international communication research dates back to the 1950s when comparative news flow studies emerged, they have a common approach. 'All empirical studies on news and television flows have been based on methodological nationalism ... in which nation-states are seen as an unchallenged departure point for analysis. This position, which was dominant in international communication studies, has been challenged by many globalisation theorists, most notably by Arjun Appadurai, who himself has been using the concept of flow, but in a broader way' (Rantanen in Thussu, 2007, p. 146). In his 1990 essay 'Disjuncture and Difference in the Global Cultural Economy' Appadurai argues that we should identify intersections among five dimensions of global cultural flow – ethnoscapes (landscapes of persons), mediascapes (which encompass the distribution of electronic media as well as the images that they produce), technoscapes (global configurations of technology), finanscapes (landscapes of global capital) and ideoscapes (which also involve images but are often directly political and have to do with state ideologies).

> These landscapes ... are the building blocks of what, extending Benedict Anderson, I would like to call 'imagined worlds', that is,

the multiple worlds which are constituted by the historically situ-
ated imaginations of persons and groups spread around the world. ...
An important fact of the world we live in today is that many persons
on the globe live in such imagined 'worlds' and not just in imagined communities, and thus are able to contest and sometimes even
subvert the 'imagined worlds' of the official mind and of the entre-
preneurial mentality that surround them.

(Appadurai, 1990, p. 297)

Transnational media consumption

Appadurai's approach that focusses on the global dimension resonates
with the critique of methodological nationalism developed primarily
by Ulrich Beck (see Beck, 2006) which has been widely discussed in
literature on transnational media and migration. For example, Andreas
Wimmer and Nina Glick Schiller argue that a methodological nationalist approach 'encompasses a culture, a polity, an economy and a
bounded social group. ... Almost no thought was given to why the
boundaries of the container society are drawn as they are and what
consequences follow from this methodological limitation of the analytical horizon – thus removing trans-border connections and processes
from the picture' (2002, p. 307). Myria Georgiou and Roger Silverstone
point out that in the debates on local, global and transnational media:

What has not been shaken off (and there has not been a real desire
to do so) is the central role of *the national* in inter-national communications. ... The study of communication flows and contra-flows
is still preoccupied with national corporations (which turn transnational or regional players), governments and national audiences.
It is obvious that we cannot, and should not, erase the nation as a
site of both political and cultural activity and regulation completely.
There remain the recalcitrance of the transnational and the instabili-
ties and movements of communication and cultural forms, whose
understanding is not reducible to the singularity of the national.

(as quoted in Thussu, 2007, p. 30; see also Mihelj, 2011)

Studies on the flow of 'non-Western' media contents into Europe
and their consumption by migrant communities began appearing in
the 1990s with the expansion of satellite broadcasting. For some, access
to television from countries of origin signalled a threat to migrants'

integration into 'host societies'. The concept of transnationalism has gained a particular meaning in research on migration. It 'refers to the increasing tendency among migrants to maintain ties with their country of origin – and thus to develop identities and social relations in multiple national contexts rather than being rooted in only one country at any given time' (Bartram et al., 2014, p. 140). In contemporary societies assimilation of migrants is no longer the sole path of integration (as discussed in Chapter 1) and questions are raised about the extent to which migrants can fully become part of the nation in their new home: 'arguably, transnationalism among individuals contributes to a process of fragmentation for the nation writ large, and to new modes of identity that bind populations across borders (rather than allowing borders merely to *divide* populations)' (ibid., p. 142, original emphasis; see also Chapter 1 of this book). For example, Hargreaves and Mahdjoub (1997) argue that in France immigration has historically been understood as a threat to national identity and Muslim minorities have been seen as particularly resistant to assimilation. France's traditionally assimilationist public policy was manifested also in the field of media; one such instance in the first half of the 1990s involved the exclusion of Arabic stations from licensed cable networks. In contrast, it proved much more difficult to control direct satellite broadcasting from Muslim countries: in 1995 survey data suggested that 21 per cent of Arabic speaking households had purchased satellite receivers compared to 4 per cent of the general population (ibid., p. 461).

Tristan Mattelart and Alec Hargreaves trace French media policies from the 1970s to the 1990s and they argue that it may appear that the attitudes of French regulators towards TV stations based in the Maghreb (North West Africa) developed significantly from the 1970s. '[W]hen the aim was to encourage the repatriation of immigrants, collaboration with Maghrebi stations was actively sought; with the advent of satellite TV in the 1990s, when the watchword had become integration, the aim was rather to contain and exclude the threat that those channels were thought to represent. At a deeper level, however, there is a strong continuity' (2014, p. 281) because the policy makers' ultimate aim remains the control of how the cultures of minorities and migrants are expressed through the medium of television. These developments were not unique to France and they pose some crucial questions. In Myria Georgiou's words: 'In mediated culture, perceptions and actions around inclusion and exclusion are produced and communicated. The question then becomes who is a member of the society and who has the right to belong, to be included and to be represented' (Georgiou in

Silverstone, 2005, p. 33). Shifts in media and cultural policies developed by European governments play a significant role in addressing this right to be represented in the media and to be heard, as argued in Chapter 1.

While policy makers have expressed an interest in the role of media in integration (or indeed assimilation), academic research on the subject has questioned some of the simplistic assumptions underlying such a policy (discussed already in relation to the creation of pan-European television broadcasting and to French media policies, see also Morley and Robins, 1995). These assumptions highlight the fragmentation of the nation and of the national public sphere that supposedly occur with increased migration and the spread of new media technologies.

> [Such arguments are] largely based on a sense of nostalgia for a public sphere where all citizens – independently of social differences – could participate on equal terms. This nostalgia, however, is problematic. There is significant evidence of the public sphere's historical limitations to include specific social groups. There have always been less equal constituencies – notably, working classes, women, ethnic and sexual minorities – whose experiences and interests have been marginalized from the dominant sphere of the public. Thus, assuming an all-encompassing and neutral sphere of public deliberation wherein all citizens participate as equals is not only fictitious, but also hegemonic.
>
> (Awad and Roth, 2011, p. 402)

The importance of self-representation in media for migrants (and for minorities) has already been alluded to. Drawing on Nancy Fraser's work, Awad and Roth suggest that:

> [C]ounter-publics provide spaces for minority groups to define and articulate their social perspective; develop alternative discourses and styles of communication; and raise their voices against injustice. Strengthened by this possibility of self-representation, minority groups can inform and challenge dominant publics and participate on more equal terms within broader spheres of deliberation. Deprived of this possibility, conversely, minority groups have their interests silenced.
>
> (ibid., p. 403)

Contrary to assumptions about migrants retreating to their segregated public spheres (or sphericules in Tod Gitlin's (1998) words), research into migrants' news consumption suggests that they tend to seek news broadly. Apart from maintaining a cultural closeness and familiarity, they also often turn to media from their countries of origin for news and current affairs because international news coverage in mainstream European media has been on a steady decline.

> When immigrant or diaspora populations are excluded as targets for nation-wide public service television, it can both reinforce their general feeling of exclusion from their present society, and reduce possibilities of pursuing their own interests as minorities. Instead, the transnational social space presents itself as an opportunity for developing enduring relations and acquiring relevant information and news.
>
> (Christiansen, 2004, p. 203)

In the 1990s sociologists and anthropologists were most interested in an interpretation of transnationalism that was linked to social formations which span borders, with ethnic diasporas being exemplary in this respect. 'One of the hallmarks of diaspora as a social form is the "triadic relationship" between (a) globally dispersed yet collectively self-identified ethnic groups, (b) the territorial states and contexts where such groups reside, and (c) the homeland states and contexts whence they or their forebears came' (Vertovec, 1999, p. 449). Studies on the media uses of diasporic communities have also flourished, and their central tenet is that migrants maintain a sense of belonging to an original homeland and negotiate that with belonging to a new 'host' country which has its different majority (national) community (Georgiou, 2007). The consumption of transnational media contents forms part of constructing an ethnic identity based on the identification with the national group of the original homeland. In her overview of the theoretical and empirical groundings of research on diaspora and media, Myria Georgiou (2007) acknowledges that a number of these studies are characterized by the previously discussed methodological nationalism. Asu Aksoy and Kevin Robins pose a highly relevant question in this respect:

> Should we try to understand transnational viewers, as some commentators do, in terms of their relation to their country of origin – that is to say, in terms of diasporic connections? Or should we consider their media practices, as other commentators have suggested, within the framework of the 'host' society – in terms of their status as 'ethnic minority' audiences...? The danger is to put migrant viewers

into one or the other national frame, rather than address the difference and distinctiveness of their transnational positioning.

(2003, p. 369)

They go on to argue that diaspora 'is a category par excellence of the national imaginary, a category that subordinates the social world to the national logic. It is no surprise that the "diasporic imagination" is isomorphic with the "national imagination", we would say, for the ideal of "imagined community" has been used as the basic template for capturing migrant experience and aspirations' (ibid., p. 371). With growing criticism of the limitations of the nation-centric perspective, arguments about the need to contextualize transnational migrants' use within a variety of contexts (including local and national ones) have recently emerged (see for example Budarick, 2014) but they are far from being prevalent in the field. Also, we need to keep in mind that migrant groups and transnational minorities (such as the Roma) are not homogeneous (see for example Tremlett, 2014). In comparison, media policy – particularly at the pan-European level – tends to be bound within the national container, with EU-level policy focussing on competition issues and leaving other aspects of media policy within the jurisdiction of individual member states (see for example Metykova, 2015).

New media technologies and transnationalization

The emergence of new media technologies has been explored in research into transnational media flows and transnational media practices. Some of the debates that have developed are reminiscent of earlier ones, for example, the dominance of major global players (such as Google) continues to be the focus of the attention of scholars (Lee, 2011; Rieder and Sire, 2014 among many others) as well as policy makers. In April 2015 the European Commission opened antitrust proceedings against Google:

[It] sent a Statement of Objections to Google alleging the company has abused its dominant position in the markets for general internet search services in the European Economic Area (EEA) by systematically favouring its own comparison shopping product in its general search results pages. The Commission's preliminary view is that such conduct infringes EU antitrust rules because it stifles competition and harms consumers.

(European Commission, 2015)

The dominance of 'Western' viewpoints in news coverage (online as well as offline) is ongoing (Himelboim et al., 2010; Peters and Broersma, 2013; Watanabe, 2013; Segev, 2015). The internet was expected to bring about a greater diversity and accessibility of media contents, partly due to its supposedly de-centralized nature, and Hesmondhalgh argues that search engines must be taken into account if we are to assess the validity of such claims. The ways in which search engines create a hierarchy of information has been discussed widely, and with the emergence of sponsored search – which enables content providers to pay for having their pages ranked higher – the issue of which contents are listed and which are excluded is crucial in assessing the quality of information. '[F]ew web users are aware of the issues involved in search rankings and many treat search engines as near-objective sources of information, much like a library catalogue' (Hesmondhalgh, 2013, p. 330). Importantly, internet searches are globally dominated by three companies – Google, Yahoo and Microsoft. In the UK in May 2015 it was reported that: 'Google enjoys the bulk of the UK search engine market share, handling 88.38% of all queries, comfortably ahead of Microsoft's Bing with 6.7% and Yahoo with 3.54%' (The Eword, 2015). This links to arguments made in earlier chapters about new media technologies not being an automatic remedy to exclusion from the mediated public sphere. It is not only search engines that cross national borders. Other online companies have also expanded globally: the online streaming of music and films has expanded significantly – Apple's music streaming service iTunes had 800 million accounts all over the world in spring 2015 and Netflix reported 62.3 million users globally in the first quarter of 2015 (Forbes, 2015).

Research has also explored the potential of online media to enable counter public spheres for migrants and minorities. Although, as Chapter 2 stressed, we need to keep in mind that the digital divide continues to be a relevant issue when we explore minorities' access to new media technologies, we find a number of studies that convincingly argue that the internet can provide a space in which counter-publics emerge. For example, Stine Eckert and Kalyani Chadha explore the case of Muslim bloggers in Germany:

[I]f expressing identity and creating community represent the type of intrapublic practices undertaken by these bloggers, their use of blogs to highlight misrepresentations of Muslims in the dominant public sphere and to create counter-discourses, demonstrates the outward orientation in their discursive repertoire. Indeed, all our interviewees maintained that, despite very few exceptions such as the national public radio Deutschlandradio or the renowned weekly newspaper *Die Zeit*, Muslims were typically stigmatized or stereotyped within the German mainstream media and that highlighting this fact was a fundamental focus of their discursive work online.

(2013, p. 934)

In conclusion they maintain that 'indeed, while we do not argue that the public sphere in Germany is becoming more expansive and inclusive of Muslims we do argue that Muslim bloggers in Germany are seeking to challenge it in new ways' (ibid., p. 940). These counter-publics are characterized by diversity, although it is sometimes suppressed in order to project producers as a unified group. Moreover, because some of these counter-publics are outward facing and 'perform' their identities towards the majority, the discourse that they promote can also be restrictive. In a study of Dutch blogs Rolien Hoyng found that:

speech codes on WBH [wijblijvenhier.nl which translates into English as westayhere.nl] not only regulate the sayable but also imply a claim to membership of, and/or representativeness regarding, the Dutch polity. ... WBH's mission is to open up dialogue in search of social cohesion on the basis of universals such as equality and tolerance. However ... on WBH it [tolerance] is understood in almost oppositional terms: as the commitment to using speech carefully and working toward mutual understanding through ongoing translation.

(2014, p. 357)

As already mentioned migrant or minority groups should not be understood as homogeneous, and the ways in which they use online media collectively also varies. Some develop online activities with the aim of bringing about political change in their countries of origin rather than focussing on issues that they face as newcomers to a country. Some empirically rich examples in this respect include research on Ethiopian journalists working from Western European countries and the United States by Skjerdal (2011); on the Tunisian diaspora's role in the diffusion of cyberactivism concerning legitimate claims for democracy and human rights by Graziano (2012); Ghorashi and Broersma (2009) on the Iranian diaspora and the alteration in its goals from political change to humanitarian help; or Ben-David (2012) whose study explores Palestinian online communities' shift from advocacy for political change to a transnational solidarity network focussed on Palestinian rights and the Boycott movement.

Research into the broader issues of migrants' everyday use of media technologies in constructing their identities and maintaining transnational ties have mushroomed, including explorations of their use of mobile technologies in transnational connections. (See for example Vancea and Olivera (2013) on the use of mobile phones in managing children of migrant mothers who live a great distance away; Wallis (2013) on Chinese migrant women's use of mobile phones; Tazanu (2015) on the role of mobile phones in channelling monetary resources to Cameroon and its implications for relationships among migrants and non-migrants; Bonini (2011) on mobile phone use and home-making.) These studies tend to be empirically rich and some also attempt to generate new theoretical insights. For example, Madianou and Miller (2011) draw on a long-term ethnographic study of prolonged separation between Filipino migrant mothers and their children and advocate the concept of polymedia that aims to capture the complex ways in which a variety of media are being combined. The term 'polymedia' is used 'to refer to these various, constantly changing media and the need for each relationship to create a configuration of usage' (p. 124). Studying media must take into account that 'each medium makes sense only within a wider environment within which it finds its niche and is defined relationally' (p. 139). Scholars have also been exploring ways in which they can overcome the 'national container' focus in research on transnational migration. Kevin Robins (2001), for example, uses the city as an analytical category when he thinks 'against the nation and through the city' (to use the title of his article) in his exploration of (super)diverse London as a city which provides an existential and experiential space in which migrants can find ways of identifying that are not as restrictive as those of the national culture/mediated public sphere. My work on migration has placed migrants' media use in the context of everyday lived experiences and routines to show how media play a role in establishing a sense of normalcy following the disruptive experience of migration (Metykova, 2010). With Shaun Moores I have explored trans-European migrants' practical and emotional relationships with their physical (and media) environments (Moores and Metykova, 2010). Scholarly attempts at overcoming the shortcomings of a national frame in research on media and transnational flows represent a relatively new phenomenon and they have not yet had an identifiable impact on policy making.

Conclusion

This chapter has explored the transformation of worldwide media industries from globalization to transnationalization. The transnationalization of media markets was not an accidental development and government policies played a significant part in the process, including those related to the marketization of the media. Attempts at correcting imbalances in the global flow of media products have also been played out within international organizations such as UNESCO, but institutionalized, policy-led efforts have failed thus far. At odds with expectations, new media technologies have not brought significant improvements in the one-way flow of news. This chapter discussed the case of Al Jazeera as the most widely recognized producer of a contra-flow in news. I have argued that in the case of European governments, economic goals have mainly been pursued in media policies, however, there have been some attempts at using media for integration purposes as well as for building a sense of European identity. The chapter has argued that migrants' and minorities' media uses need to be approached in a complex manner and not read merely as an indication of a willingness or indeed a reluctance or outright refusal to integrate. In other words, discussions should concentrate on the unique positioning of transnational media users rather than on their diasporic or ethnic minority status. Policy makers' simplistic understanding of the effects of media combined with a narrow nation-bound understanding of identity has resulted in some policies being formulated in a misguided way. Nonetheless, the focus on the national framework has also characterized academic studies on transnational media (and their uses), as the concept of methodological nationalism explains. The chapter has discussed attempts at overcoming this shortcoming in studies on transnational migrants' media uses, yet these are arguably a relatively recent development. Government policies related to media and the integration of migrants and minorities have been crucial in enabling the participation of these groups in the mediated public sphere. The chapter has shown that, although new media technologies may be utilized by minority groups to create spaces in which they act as counter publics, the technology enhanced opportunities are not devoid of issues of hierarchy and inequality and the situation is complicated by the minority groups' attempts at relating to the minority as well as the majority populations.

5 Diversity and Media Producers

I have discussed the importance of a diversity of voices and views in the public sphere in previous chapters. In order to achieve this desirable goal, I argue that we need a variety of producers who make contents and thus make their voices – and the voices of those they represent – heard. This chapter explores thinking on the influence of the characteristics of media producers – above all their gender and ethnicity – on the contents that they make. The underlying concern is that the lack of media professionals with certain characteristics and opinions leads to the silencing of some groups in society or their misrepresentation in media. It is impossible to discuss media professionals and their characteristics in general in a chapter of this length so I will focus on professional journalists because of the particular social and democratic roles bestowed on this profession and especially because of the possible influence of their gender and ethnicity on the contents that they produce.

We might make the assumption that if we have large numbers of women and representatives of ethnic minorities working as journalists, their voices will be well represented in the public sphere. This assumption is not a new one and it has been developed in scholarship and also at the centre of policy making for some time.

A historical example that continues to be highly relevant involves the lack of African-American journalists working in US media and its subsequent influence on the portrayal of African Americans. The severity of the situation and its possible consequences were, for example, discussed by the National Advisory Commission on Civil Disorders (known as the Kerner Commission) appointed by President Lyndon B. Johnson to investigate the causes of the 1960s race riots. The report pointed out that '[f]ewer than 5 percent of the people employed by the news business in editorial jobs in the United States today are Negroes. Fewer than 1 percent of editors and supervisors are Negroes, and most of them work for Negro-owned organizations ... The plaint is "We can't find qualified Negroes." But this rings hollow from an industry where, only yesterday, jobs were scarce and promotion unthinkable for a man whose skin was black.' The report went on to argue that the hiring of token African-American journalists was insufficient in addressing the problem because 'newspaper and television policies are, generally speaking, not set by reporters. Editorial decisions about which stories to cover and which to use are made by editors. Yet, very few Negroes in this country are involved in making these decisions, because very few, if any, supervisory editorial jobs are held by Negroes' (Kerner, 1968, Chapter XV). The report's section on media addressed the heart of the problem – it is not sufficient to increase the number of journalists belonging to ethnic minority groups in itself, it is crucial that they occupy positions of power in media organizations.

Quantitative increases in the number of minority journalists in US newsrooms have been monitored by scholars as well as professional organizations and activists. In 1978 the American Society of Newspaper Editors (a non-profit professional organization founded in 1922 and renamed the American Society of News Editors in 2009) challenged the newspaper industry to achieve racial parity by the year 2000. While this appears to have been a realistic objective in the light of expected developments in the industry, 'in its essence this goal seems somewhat disturbing, for such proclamations tend to obscure another side of the issue, indicated by the question: What should be the role of Black journalists in the news media?' (Mapp, 1979, p. 10; see also Terry, 2007; Wilson, 1991).

This brief historical detour is illustrative of the complex questions that I aim to explore in this chapter. First, the chapter considers the role of journalists in democratic societies and that in the context of journalists' perceptions of their own professional standing and practices and the context of different journalistic traditions. The chapter interrogates the extent to which journalists can be led by their personal beliefs and characteristics in the selection and production of news. The chapter then moves on to consider the cases of gender and ethnicity in relation to practitioners of professional journalism. Three inter-related phenomena are considered: the gap in the number of women and ethnic minority journalists in the profession; the social construction of gender and ethnicity within news organizations; and the possibility that women and ethnic minority journalists have a divergent understanding of the role of journalism in society and the particular professional values and practices that guide it.

Journalists and their profession

Chapter 2 suggested the importance of news and current affairs when understanding the democratic roles of media. We can think of examples of individual journalists who achieved significant fame for their investigations: Bob Woodward and Carl Bernstein of *The Washington Post* who in 1972 broke the Watergate story; more recently the award winning foreign correspondent Marie Colvin who was killed in Syria in 2012 or Glenn Greenwald and Laura Poitras whose work on surveillance by the National Security Agency received prestigious awards in 2014. However, we should keep in mind that journalists (and other media content producers) operate within a particular professional field and inside media organizations that have a greater influence on the conduct of their work than their personal characteristics and convictions. This is despite the fact that journalists' personal characteristics (and especially political convictions) tend to be a recurrent theme when considering bias or inequalities in news outputs. Conservative critics in particular have repeatedly referred to a liberal bias in the news media which is supposedly the consequence of the overall tendency of journalists to hold left-leaning views. (In the UK the BBC has been accused of left-wing bias repeatedly, see for example Simons, 2013; in the US the increase in the public's perception of a liberal bias in the media has been linked to increased claims of such bias by conservative elites, see for example Watts et al., 1999; Smith, 2010.) While surveys of journalists have provided evidence of a prevalence of left-leaning views, the most recent study in the American Journalist series found that '[c]ompared with 2002, the percentage of full-time U.S. journalists who claim to be Democrats has dropped 8 percentage points in 2013 to about 28 percent, moving this figure closer to the overall population percentage of 30 percent. ... This is the lowest percentage of journalists saying they are Democrats since 1971' (Willnat and Weaver, 2014, p. 11). The study goes on to present some surprising results:

> An even larger drop was observed among journalists who said they were Republicans in 2013 (7.1 percent) than in 2002 (18 percent), but the 2013 figure is still notably lower than the percentage of U.S. adults who identified with the Republican Party (24 percent according to the poll mentioned above). About half of all journalists (50.2 percent) said they were Independents, which is 10 percentage points above the figure for all U.S. adults (40 percent). Overall, U.S. journalists today are much more likely to identify themselves as

Independents rather than Democrats or Republicans – a pattern not observed before 2002.

(ibid.)

The arguments about liberal (or leftist) journalistic bias are opposed by many journalists as well as academics who argue that professional journalistic practices and values (such as objectivity, balance and fairness) help prevent journalists from displaying potential personal biases in their work. We should, however, remember that the professional journalistic values and practices that this chapter refers to are ideal ones, and journalists negotiate these in the course of their work. Also, importantly, debates about the nature of these values and their impact on journalistic contents are nuanced and I can only sketch out the main contours of these here. (For a more detailed discussion, particularly on journalistic objectivity see for example Schudson, 1995, 2001 and 2003; Broersma, 2010; Maras, 2012; Blaagaard, 2013.)

So how do journalists understand their role in society and what values guide their professional conduct? In *The American Journalist in the 1990s* David Weaver and G. Cleveland Wilhoit (1996) introduced a three-fold classification of journalists' self-conception of their roles in society: interpreter – journalists who see themselves primarily as interpreters think that the most important aspect of their profession is the analysis and interpretation of complex questions; disseminator – the most important aspect of a journalist's work is to get information to the public quickly; adversary – journalists who carry out critical investigations of government and business. We can also think of journalism as a shared professional ideology. In other words, we can explore how journalists give meaning to their work in the newsrooms and investigate their system of professional beliefs about their occupation. Mark Deuze suggests that:

In decades of journalism studies, scholars refer to the journalists' professionalization process as a distinctly ideological development, as the emerging ideology served to continuously refine and reproduce a consensus about who was a 'real' journalist, and what (parts of) news media at any time would be considered examples of 'real' journalism. These evaluations shift subtly over time; yet always serve to maintain the dominant sense of what is (and should be) journalism.

(2005, p. 444)

He goes on to identify five ideal-typical traits or values that are part of journalists' occupational ideology: public service, objectivity, autonomy, immediacy and ethics. Journalists provide a public service as watchdogs or 'newshounds'; they are active collectors and disseminators of information who have a sense of immediacy, actuality and speed (inherent in the concept of 'news'). Importantly they are impartial, neutral, objective, fair and (thus) credible, and they also must be autonomous, free and independent in their work. Finally, journalists have a sense of ethics, validity and legitimacy (ibid.). Deuze's revisiting of the 'old concept' of occupational ideology leads him to conclude that theories of what journalism is and what it could be miss two crucial elements – technology and multiculturalism. I will return to multiculturalism later in the chapter when exploring whether ethnic minority journalists conceptualize their roles in society in a distinctive way.

While we find different traditions of journalism and different social, economic and political conditions under which the profession operates in different democratic societies, the above core values tend to apply in general. Objectivity, for example, played a key role in the professionalization of US journalism (see for example Chalaby, 1996; Schudson, 2001), and the so-called US/Anglo-American or liberal model of professional journalism – characterized by objectivity and detachment – is becoming dominant in European democracies, although French and Italian journalists have traditionally prioritized opinion over reportage in their news production (see Esser and Umbricht, 2013, cf. Hallin and Mancini, 2004). There are, of course, forms of alternative journalism that are guided by a different set of values (see for example Harcup, 2005 and 2011; Waltz, 2005; Bailey et al., 2007; Fisher, 2015) but these fall outside the scope of this chapter and the argument that I am making here. The question that follows is that if mainstream news producers are neutral and detached professionals, particularly if they are also increasingly guided by concerns related to living in culturally diverse societies as Deuze (2005) argues, do we need a more diverse body of professional journalists to achieve a more balanced coverage of news? Before we explore this question, we should consider who determines what contents get into the media and how they do it, and the concept of gatekeeping is relevant in this respect.

In 1949 David Manning White conducted what became a classic 'gatekeeping study' (1950). His research targeted an editor at a small daily newspaper and in particular the process by which he selected news stories from those sent to him by news agencies. White concluded that the selection process – in the course of which the editor rejected 90 per cent of the stories – was highly subjective.

> In its simplest conceptualization within mass communication, gatekeeping is the process by which the vast array of potential news messages are winnowed, shaped, and prodded into those few that are actually transmitted by the news media. It is often defined as a series of decision points at which news items are either continued or halted as they pass along news channels from source to reporter to a series of editors. However, the gatekeeping process is also thought of as consisting of more than just selection, to include how messages are shaped, timed for dissemination, and handled. In fact, gatekeeping in mass communication can be seen as the overall process through which the social reality transmitted by the news media is constructed, and is not just a series of 'in' and 'out' decisions.
> (Shoemaker et al., 2001, p. 233; see also Shoemaker and Vos, 2009)

Further studies pointed out that editors' choices were not entirely subjective but rather they were guided by organizational and institutional influences, and news values (such as drama/surprise, importance/relevance/magnitude, entertainment, proximity, negativity/bad news) played an important role. (The study of news values originated in the 1960s with Johan Galtung and Mari Holmboe Ruge playing a pivotal role, see Galtung and Ruge, 1965.) Gatekeeping continues to be an area of interest in research on news production and it appears that journalistic routines rather than individual characteristics or beliefs drive the selection of news, although Shoemaker et al. (2001) suggest that more research is required on other factors that impact on the selection process, including at the organizational level (profitability, for example). The spread of online news production and consumption has seen audiences playing an increasing role in the selection of news items for coverage, and hence researchers began exploring their role in the gatekeeping process. For example, Singer (2014) argues that website users can be understood as secondary gatekeepers while Tandoc (2014) proposes a model for understanding the role of web analytics in the gatekeeping process. These explorations of gatekeeping suggest an increasingly complex picture of editorial practices, yet they do not indicate that we need to reconsider the role of journalists' personal preferences and beliefs in gatekeeping.

Women journalists

Journalists' personal beliefs and characteristics thus appear to be less important than professional routines and values in the process of news selection and news production. Yet this does not mean that various groups in society are fairly represented in the media and the case of gender sheds light on reasons for such imbalances. Studies on gender and professional journalism have gained more attention globally since the 1990s and they have been developed within academia as well as by a variety of governmental (including global actors such as the UN) and non-governmental organizations that advocate equality for women. (These organizations include the Global Media Monitoring Project, which runs a global quantitative study *Who Makes the News* every five years, and the Women's Media Centre that focusses on the US and combines campaigns with media training.) In order to capture the complexity that characterizes the experiences of women journalists, this chapter considers three inter-related aspects:

- the gender gap in news journalism which involves the numbers of men and women working in news media, the pay they receive as well as the positions they occupy in media organizations;
- the gendering of media organizations – organizations are not gender neutral;
- the gendered nature of the journalistic profession, exploring whether journalistic values and routines are gender neutral or whether – as some argue – female journalists understand professional ideology in a distinctive manner.

In 1998 Liesbet van Zoonen proposed that, although news journalism is not the only profession in which men dominate,

> [T]he debate about women in journalism has taken on an additional relevance, however, because of the particular tasks and requirements of journalism in democratic societies, one of which is believed to be the production and distribution of balanced and fair information. ... Because the news is made by men, it is thought to reflect the interests and values of men too, and therefore news cannot serve very well the needs of this famous other fifty percent of the population, namely women.
>
> (p. 34)

Van Zoonen's argument continues to be relevant as research from a variety of countries over periods of time confirms a gender gap in journalism. According to the previously mentioned study by Willnat and Weaver, writing in 2014:

> the percentage of female U.S. journalists has increased from 33 percent in 2002 to 37.5 percent in 2013. However, women still represent only slightly more than one-third of all full-time journalists working for the U.S. news media, as has been true since the early 1980s. This trend persists despite the fact that more women than ever are graduating from journalism schools. ... Compared to the U.S. civilian work force in 2012, U.S. journalists are considerably less likely to be women (37.5 percent vs. 46.9 percent) and even less likely than the overall U.S. managerial and professional work force, which included 51.5 percent women in 2012. Thus, retention of women in journalism is still a problem.
>
> (2014, p. 6)

It is important to pay attention to the fact that the quantitative gender gap persists despite the fact that more women than ever before gain university degrees in journalism. For example, in the UK '[t]here are regularly more women than men studying journalism on a full-time undergraduate basis in the UK, according to data ... [from] the Universities and Colleges Admissions Service (UCAS). The figures from 2007 to 2014 show the number of women on courses outnumber men in every year except 2008, when the numbers are equal' (Reid, 2015).

We should also remember that the number of women training to become journalists or even employed in journalism does not in itself tell us anything about the power and prestige that female journalists enjoy in news media, and hence about what control they can exercise in the process of news selection and news production. Despite the fact that more women obtain university education in journalism and can hence expect to be financially better off, the gender pay gap has not disappeared. For example, in the US,

> Female journalists with more than 20 years of work experience earn 6.6 percent less on average than their male colleagues with the same level of experience ($72,679/$67,885). However, for journalists with 15 to 19 years ($53,333/$41,944) and 10 to 14 years of experience ($40,000/$31,429) the income gap jumps to 21.4 percent. Among journalists with five to nine years of experience, the gap shrinks to 2.4 percent ($31,293/$30,555) and then reverses for those with less than five years of work experience ($24,167/$25,761).
>
> (Willnat and Weaver, 2014, p. 6)

Moreover, research consistently shows that women tend to work in areas of journalism that are considered less prestigious (in local as opposed to national newspapers); as news presenters rather than news reporters and in so-called soft news rather than hard news that involve politics and economics (see for example van Zoonen, 1998; de Bruin and Ross, 2004; Gill, 2007; and also reports by non-profit organizations such as the World Association for Christian Communication's Global Media Monitoring Project and 'The Status of Women in US Media 2014' report by the Women's Media Centre).

The lack of women in managerial positions in media organizations (particularly in top management roles) has also been the subject of much debate and research. For example, Eleanor Mills – editorial director of *The Sunday Times* in the UK – points out that:

> The last woman to edit a daily broadsheet was Rosie Boycott at *The Independent* from January to April 1998. The deep end of most newspapers – by which I mean news, comment, the backbench – is still overwhelmingly male. A recent WIJ [Women in Journalism] survey of front-page bylines found that between 75 per cent and 90 per cent (depending on the paper, with the *Financial Times* and *The Independent* the worst) were written by men. The average ratio of male to female bylines is 78:22.
>
> (2014, p. 17)

Indeed, very few prominent female journalists come to mind when one is prompted. However, among those is most likely to be Jill Abramson, who acted as executive director of the *New York Times* between 2011 and 2014, and in the UK Katherine Viner, the editor of *The Guardian* who took up this position in 2015. The scope of this chapter does not allow a historically informed discussion about the changing roles of women in professional journalism (see for example Chambers et al., 2004; Rush et al., 2004; Fahs, 2011; specifically on women at the BBC see Chapter 9 in Seaton, 2015). However, we should not think about historical developments as linear or as a progression from a situation less favourable to women in journalism to one that is more favourable.

Gender segregation in the labour market has been a long-term concern and in the media industries a distinction has been made between horizontal and vertical segregation. Gill (2007) describes horizontal segregation as 'the way that media industries and the different roles within them are segmented along gender lines, with women concentrated in low-status parts of the industry (e.g. local papers and women's magazines) and in particular types of role (e.g. administration and support)' and vertical segregation as 'a way of capturing the fact that even when in the same general field (e.g. television production) they [women] tend to be concentrated at lower points in the hierarchy, while men dominate senior management' (p. 121). 'Where are the Women?', a 2014 report by the Nieman Foundation, collated research findings on the position of women in a variety of US newsrooms:

> Despite making up half the population, and more than half of communication school graduates each year, women represent just 35 percent of newspaper supervisors, according to the 2014 American Society of News Editors (ASNE) newsroom census. They run just three of the nation's 25 largest titles, eight of the 25 biggest papers with circulations under 100,000, and three of the 25 biggest with circulations under 50,000. Only one of the top 25 international titles is run by a woman.
>
> The numbers also are skewed in radio and TV. In a 2014 Radio Television Digital News Association (RTDNA) survey, women made up just 31 percent of TV news directors and 20 percent of general managers, despite making up more than 40 percent of the TV workforce. The same survey found that women accounted for just 23 percent of radio news directors and 18 percent of general managers.
>
> (Griffin, 2014)

The report goes on to argue that the picture is equally skewed globally. 'The Global Report on the Status of Women in the News Media surveyed more than 500 media companies in almost 60 countries, and found that men occupied 73 percent of the top management jobs' (Griffin, 2014).

The glass ceiling in the media industries (see Falk and Grizard, 2005; Franks, 2013) continues to exist also in countries that have a long-existing reputation for, and well developed legal instruments ensuring, gender equality. Monika Djerf-Pierre (2005) acknowledges that Nordic countries are rightly noted for their high level of gender equality and that almost 50 per cent of Swedish journalists are women, but the picture changes when one explores the top management level of media organizations – the media elite – with about 26 per cent of the elite positions in the media held by women. In her analysis Djerf-Pierre builds on Bourdieu's theory of capital, and she 'think[s] of gender as a specific form of capital, where female gender is often negative and male is positive capital'. However, she also recognizes 'that the negative gender capital can be countered by amassing other types of capital. ... It can be

presupposed that if women in the media elite do possess more professional, cultural, economic or social capital of a particular type than their
male counterpart, this may serve as an indicator of a specific form of
capital that counterbalances the negative capital of femaleness' (p. 272).

Importantly, Djerf-Pierre concludes that it is crucial to bear in mind
that in all elite groups 'positions that are acquired through various (open)
electoral processes have a higher degree of female representation (as does
the political field in general). ... The active gender and equality policies
of the Swedish political system have positively influenced the media
field and ... better gender representation in certain sectors of the media
is partly a result of an activist gender policy' (p. 281). She also stresses
that the role of public service broadcasters should not be underestimated
in this respect because 'they are under heavy political pressure to imple-
ment these policies and, since the mid-1970s, public service radio and
television have been actively promoting gender equality at all levels of
the organizations. Perceived in this way, politics does matter when it
comes to gender representation, in the media and elsewhere' (ibid.).

Gendered news organizations and practices

It is clear from the previous section that the gender gap in journalism
persists globally. However, in addressing this gap we need to focus not
only on the presence and roles of women in the media industries but
we also need to understand and explore the gendered nature of news
organizations and the actual negotiation and practising of gender at
work. The key for exploring arguments about the gendering of the
workplace is that gender is socially constructed, that is, society creates
gender roles that are prescribed as appropriate for a person of a given
gender. As a consequence, gender is dynamic and is constructed and
negotiated in social interaction (see for example Lorber and Farrell,
1991). Although organizations – not only media ones – are guided by
codes of professional conduct and internal rules and regulations which
may impact on the women working in them (for example, guidelines
relating to non-discrimination and provision of childcare), importantly, research on the social construction of gender in organizations,
'documents dynamics that are implicit and unconscious rather than
active and intentional' (Foldy, 2012, p. 499).

> Most researchers do not suggest that individual employees are
> explicitly trying to modify either their gender or racial identity; nor

do they suggest that organizations are deliberately trying to recast these identities. However, overall, the research does suggest that organizations contribute to the construction of both gender and race, even without the intention to do so.

(ibid.)

Patricia Martin (2003) proposes a similar argument when stating that 'as men engage in gendering practices consistent with institution-alized norms and stereotypes of masculinity, they nonetheless create social closure and oppression' (p. 360). And she goes on to explain that:

If women simply go along with institutionalized norms and stereo-types of femininity, they remain outside of men's informal networks and usually formal ones too. ... Yet women who practice femininity according to femininity stereotypes that define women as subor-dinate may gain approval from men, but they do not gain equal status. ... Women who fail to practice femininity according to femi-ninity stereotypes that define women as subordinate lose approval and end up with even lower status than they would otherwise. ... Men who practice masculinity/masculinities according to mascu-linity stereotypes that define men as dominant do gain approval and status from men. While such men may not gain approval from women, their hold over powerful positions gives women no alternative but to respect them, especially in work situations where women's opportunities are at stake.

(ibid.)

It is thus not surprising that the term 'old boys' club' has been used to describe women's marginalization in news journalism (see for example Byerly, 2013; North, 2014).

The final issue that this chapter considers in relation to gender and journalism is whether women practise journalism as a profession in a distinctive manner. Van Zoonen (1998, p. 36) identifies areas in which the gendered nature of the profession (or in other words, areas in which 'feminine values' in professional journalism) are demonstrated, and some of these are linked to the definition of newsworthiness: selec-tion of topics and angles (women journalists are concerned about the lack of topics relevant to women), choice of sources (men journalists tend to rely on male sources) and ethical values (men journalists are perceived as detached and insensitive). These areas have been subjected to research (for a literature review on women's selection and use of sources see for example Zoch and VanSlyke Turk, 1998), and studies have also considered journalistic fields that are traditionally heavily dominated by men (such as sports journalism, see for example Schoch, 2013; on token female sports journalists see for example Hardin and Whiteside, 2009 and reports relating to the US by The Institute for Diversity and Ethics in Sport available at http://www.tidesport.org/). However, research on the influence of gender on news products and the process of news production has been inconclusive thus far. Lavie and Lehman-Wilzig (2009) have pointed out that one possible reason for inconsistencies in such research is the use of exclusively quantitative or qualitative research methods rather than a combination of these.

> [They] conclude that editorial respondents' declarations should be viewed as a product of a specific social environment, thus demanding of the researcher a critical – perhaps even sceptical – approach vis-a-vis their answers, similar to reading autobiographies, memoirs and historical texts. ... However, studies that rely exclusively on content analysis of the editorial product should also be approached with great caution, for they do not reflect the complex, news decision-making process between workers specifically nor of organizational influences in general. ... The practical significance of this from a research perspective is to negate the traditional methodological approach of relying either exclusively on news professionals' declarations or solely on content analysis of the news. In other words, creating the delicate cloth of gender and the news requires not only great caution but also interlacing the warp of declarations with the woof of content analysis.
>
> (p. 84)

When reassessing research on gender and news selection and production Hanitzsch and Hanusch (2012) suggest that the influence of gender (or as they term it, the gender determination hypothesis) is problematic largely due to reasons that van Zoonen outlined in her 1998 publication:

> First, it assumes that journalists have sufficient autonomy to perform in a uniquely individual manner. Second, it rests on the belief that women journalists are distinguished more by their femininity than by any other dimension of identity, like professionalism or ethnicity. There is no consensus over the extent to which gender matters in the process of news production. Evidence is ambiguous

and often dependent on whether results are based on journalists' self-declarations or actual content. While most surveys of journalists have not been able to present substantial differences, content analyses do point to gender-related patterns.

(p. 258)

The critical point, they argue, is whether 'these differences really constitute a "feminization" of news that is driven by the growing number of women journalists, or if they simply reflect general changes in the media that are largely unrelated to gender effects. ...The causal relationship between journalism and gender might actually work in the opposite direction: the ongoing transformation of news-making may open up journalism as a profession for women' (ibid.). Hanitzsch and Hanusch conclude that '[n]either of the three levels of analysis – individual, newsroom and sociocultural – showed meaningful or strong patterns of gender differences. ... Thus, a major conclusion of this study is that a journalist's gender alone is not a significant determinant of journalists' professional views' (ibid., p. 274).

The discussion on the influence of gender on news selection and production has highlighted the role of ideal typical professional values in journalism that are understood as more influential on the outcome of journalistic work than journalists' gender or personal convictions. However, women continue to be marginalized in journalism both in terms of their numbers in the profession and in the types of positions that they occupy. I have also argued that in order to understand the marginalization of women in journalism, we need to take into account the less evident processes of the social construction of gender in media organizations. Perhaps the most intriguing question is that of the gendered nature of journalistic practices and values. Although the evidence gathered so far is inconclusive, the suggestion that women may perceive their professional roles and values differently from men raises important questions about the limitations of our understanding and practice of professional journalism.

The case of ethnicity

The remaining part of this chapter turns its attention to ethnicity and argues that journalists of ethnic minority backgrounds are in many ways in a similar position to that of women. Race factors heavily in income inequality, journalists of minority backgrounds are under-represented in positions of power and race is socially constructed in the workplace. However, I explore an additional issue that ethnic minority journalists face in their work and that is the expectation that they will act as a bridge between the majority and minority populations and enable the better integration of ethnic minority groups.

Let us first consider the quantitative gap. If the American Society of Newspaper Editors' goal from 1978 mentioned in the opening of this chapter did not become a reality by 2000, had it done so by the early 2010s? According to the 2010 US census 36.3% of the US population belong to a racial or ethnic minority group and data from 2013 suggest that 13.2% of the US population is Black or African American (Census 2014, 2015). The 2014 American Society of News Editors (ASNE) report stated that minority employment in US daily newspapers was 13.34% (compared to 3.95% in 1978, see ASNE, 2015). The employment figures for US broadcast media are somewhat higher. According to 2013 data published by the Radio Television Digital News Association/Hofstra University, 'the minority workforce in TV news, at 22.4%, [is] the highest it's been in 13 years and the second highest level ever. ... Still, as far as minorities are concerned, the bigger picture remains unchanged. In the last 24 years, the minority population in the U.S. has risen 11 points; but the minority workforce in TV news is up less than half that (4.6), and the minority workforce in radio is up 2.2' (RTDNA, 2015). Following the economic recession, the trends in the employment of ethnic minority journalists have been of concern in the US as well as the UK:

> The number of black journalists working at U.S. daily newspapers has dropped 40% since 1997, according to the latest data from the American Society of News Editors. That represents a loss of almost 1,200 journalists – from 2,946 in 1997 to 1,754 in 2013. It's also a steeper decline than the rate of job losses for white journalists – a 34% decrease during the same time period. In the last 16 years, the ranks of Hispanic and Asian journalists have also declined, though not as steeply – losing 13% and 2%, respectively.
>
> (Anderson, 2014)

The UK's Creative Skillset annual report for 2013/14 noted the 'alarming decline in Black, Asian and Minority Ethnic (BAME) people in the Creative Industries from 6.7% in 2009 to 5.4% in 2012' (Creative Skillset, undated, p. 5). In comparison according to 2011 Census data, 14% of the UK's population belonged to other than white ethnic groups (ONS, 2015).

When we look at the representation of ethnic minorities in the management of media companies, the picture gets even bleaker (see for example the above mentioned reports by the American Society of Newspaper Editors, the Radio Television Digital News Association and the Pew Research Center). Ethnic minority journalists face similar types of marginalization in the news industries to women. When it comes to leadership, statistical data paint a rather gloomy picture: in the 2015 census by the American Society of Newspaper Editors there were '12 percent of participating organizations saying at least one of their top three editors is a person of color' (ASNE 2015a). The National Association of Black Journalists (NABJ) arrived at a similar conclusion about the ratio of minority journalists working in managerial positions in television newsrooms (NABJ, 2015). As in the case of women, studies on ethnic minority journalists raise questions about the ways in which professional practices and values may actually contribute to the marginalization of ethnic minority groups. It has been argued convincingly that news values represent the power hierarchy and skew the representation of minorities but because they are the foundation of professional journalism it is very difficult for African American journalists in the US, for example, to challenge them (see Wilson, 2000).

As already mentioned, Deuze (2005) argues that journalists operate in culturally diverse societies and hence they have to develop an active awareness of the needs of culturally diverse publics. However, it appears that media organizations may attempt to build such awareness by hiring token ethnic minority journalists or assigning 'minority interest topics' to them. In their 2007 study David Pritchard and Sarah Stonbely echo Mapp's concerns quoted in the opening of this chapter:

Having minority journalists writing mostly about relatively power-less segments of society, while white journalists write mostly about powerful institutions, may have a certain logic, given that people of colour are overrepresented among the powerless and whites over-represented among the powerful. To the extent that such practices exist, however, they both reinforce white dominance in newsrooms and shed light on the social processes by which white dominance is perpetuated.

(p. 232)

They go on to argue that being assigned to cover minority-related topics may in itself be detrimental to the career development of minority journalists because '[w]ithin American newspapers, government and business beats are widely considered the fastest tracks to management positions' (ibid.). Pritchard and Stonbely have provocatively titled their article 'Racial Profiling in the Newsroom' and, while they identified race as an influence on the assignment of stories, they acknowledge that they did not detect overtly racist attitudes in the newsroom. What did, however, strike them was:

> the invisibility of whiteness in discussions about the bases for story assignments. The journalists, whatever their race, spoke of racial diversity only when they were talking about minority reporters and minority-oriented topics. The hegemony of whiteness was such that none of the journalists appeared to have thought about the role of whiteness in the coverage of the largely white realms of politics and business.
>
> (ibid., p. 244)

This leads them to conclude that 'the implicit notion was that minority reporters get their assignments because of their race, while white reporters get theirs because of hard work and talent. Such thinking keeps journalists of colour at the margins of news creation and newsroom decision making' (ibid.).

How do journalists of ethnic minority backgrounds negotiate the expectations that they face at work in terms of being responsible for diversity coverage or speaking outright for the integration of minorities with the expectations of professional ideology? Chapter 2 discussed the special roles that are fulfilled by minority media but we need to bear in mind that ethnic minority journalists can face specific expectations also in mainstream media. What has been suggested by Pritchard and Stonbely in the case of US newsrooms, also applies to European countries where ethnic minority journalists face ghettoization. The responses that Gunila Hultén solicited from journalists-immigrants in Sweden are typical in this respect: 'When you're an immigrant you think: do I get this gig just because I'm an immigrant and am expected to write about the suburbs and all that crap? So when I got this job I asked [editor] did I get this job just because you need a blatte [someone of immigrant background]?' (2009, p. 8). Another journalist expressed these concerns: 'But you have to realize that just because I have a different background it doesn't mean that I have more immigrant friends than you do. I don't come from Rosengråd or Södertällje or Akalla [areas with large immigrant populations], you see. I don't have those contacts. ... And that scares me sometimes. What is expected of me?' (ibid.).

We do not only need to consider the expectation of writing about certain topics or having access to certain sources that complicates ethnic minority journalists' professional self-perceptions. Ethnic minority journalists – regardless of whether they are employed in mainstream media or in those targeting ethnic minorities in particular – are sometimes expected to promote the integration of ethnic minorities by their employers or colleagues, and sometimes they adopt a kind of 'bridging' position between the ethnic minority to which they belong and the majority. In their study of ethnic minority journalists in Germany, Anne-Katrin Arnold and Beate Schneider (2007) found that journalists of Turkish origin ascribed themselves, and their work, some influence on the integration of Turks in Germany.

> The specific interests of the Turkish minority rank high on their journalistic agenda. Although their first duty is neutral reporting in any case, they feel strongly obliged to report on the life of Turks living with the German majority, to expressing Turkish opinions and attitudes, and to addressing problems facing the minority. Journalists working for a Turkish medium published in Germany, though, feel somewhat less obligated to objectivity and slightly more to take the Turkish populations' side. With a somewhat defensive overall attitude, the journalists get involved critically with grievances concerning the cohabitation of the minority and majority as well as the minority's rights. The central point of their journalistic work is giving voice to their fellow Turks – this attitude is stronger among journalists with Turkish media.
>
> (p. 131)

A study on Russian speaking journalists in Estonia found that 'journalists working in Russian-language media are not too positive about their ability to promote the interests of the Russophone minority. Instead, they are more oriented towards general professional standards and their role as mediators between Estonian and Russian communities within existing possibilities' (Jufereva and Lauk, 2015, p. 63). In the words of a journalist interviewed for the project: 'Our apparent role is to connect the two communities. We are sitting on two chairs simultaneously. On the one hand, we have to keep an eye on what is going on in Russia, and we should tell people about that. On the other hand, it is necessary that we observe how the Russian-speaking community interacts with the Estonian speaking one. How realistic this role is, is another issue' (ibid., p. 62).

My research on Roma media and journalists in the Czech Republic highlighted a number of issues that journalists who belong to ethnic minorities face in their professional conduct, and Roma journalists represent an unusual case. The Roma are Europe's largest ethnic minority (an estimated ten to twelve million Roma live in the countries of the EU) that is transnational (that is, they do not have a territorial state in which they form a majority) and comprise arguably the most discriminated against minority in Europe (see for example '2011 EU Framework for National Roma Integration Strategies up to 2020' (European Commission, 2011) and 'Decade of Roma inclusion 2005–2015', www .romadecade.org). There are very few Roma journalists working in the Czech Republic (Richard Samko, a television editor and host is probably the most visible) and I have interviewed some of those working for the Czech public service radio's Roma newsroom, Roma language newspapers and magazines (such as *Romano Hangos* and *Romano Vodi*) and web-based media (Radio rota, romea.cz). I restrict my discussion here to aspects that impact on Roma journalists' professional practice and ideology. One of the most important factors in how Roma media operate is how journalists conceive their professional roles and the role of the medium for which they work. I should stress here that most of my interviewees have not trained as journalists (or completed a university degree in journalism or media) yet they spoke about ideal journalistic values at great length. They were adamant about seeking the truth and providing truthful information to the Roma about their community and the society at large, but also importantly about representing the Roma to the majority population. In some cases Roma journalists viewed their work more as advocacy and social service rather than as objective and distanced reporting. There was only one exception, a young female Roma journalist who was very open about wanting to break out of the roles typecast for the Roma. She was not interested in being an advocate for the Roma in her work, she wanted to run a high-quality family-oriented magazine for the Roma. The Czech public service radio as well as newspapers and magazines that are supported with funding from non-governmental organizations and from the Czech government are involved in a balancing act – they attempt to speak to the Roma minority and also to that segment of the majority population that is interested in Roma issues. This is reflected not only in the choice of topics that are covered but also in the languages used (with Czech often dominating). Importantly, the Roma journalists I spoke to did not reflect on this as an 'imbalance' that they had to negotiate within the framework of their professional values. Those working at the Czech public service radio were rather glad that they had found a 'safe niche' where they could work while those working in other media were concerned about the impact of funding cuts.

The negotiations of journalistic objectivity with other pressing concerns of Roma journalists in the Czech Republic highlight an issue with journalistic objectivity and trust. If Roma journalists utilize the same objective journalistic values and practices as their counterparts from the majority population, will they not contribute to the existing misrepresentations in news (for example, reporting that involves the Roma tends to relate to crime, antisocial behaviour and poverty)? Isabel Awad, for instance, argues that adhering to principles of journalistic objectivity will not necessarily address the disconnection between mainstream news and minority populations and will not empower minority groups because it is linked to existing power structures in society. The question for journalists is how to represent cultural difference when their professional values and practices are supposed to be acultural. Awad suggests that journalism needs to be involved in discussions with other fields (social sciences and humanities) that have been adjusting to the crisis of representation since the 1970s. 'A serious engagement with on-going discussions in these fields would substantially enrich the news media's approach to minority groups. It would force journalism to question realist notions of representation and essentialist notions of cultural difference. Furthermore, it would reveal that "good intentions and literary inventions cannot compensate alone for massive inequalities in the conditions of communication"' (Awad, 2011, p. 528; quoting Thomas McCarthy).

Conclusion

This chapter has outlined the continuing importance of professional ideology in explorations of the practices and values of professional journalists. It has reviewed a wide range of research on the impact of journalists' personal characteristics, beliefs and attitudes on the news selection and production process to argue that journalistic routines and possibly other factors – organizational and audience-related ones in particular – dominate in news selection rather than individual journalist's preferences or characteristics. The chapter has considered the cases of gender and ethnicity to provide a more nuanced understanding of why and how women and members of ethnic minority groups who work as professional journalists are marginalized in news media organizations. Long-term quantitative data document the persistent gaps in the numbers of women and ethnic minority journalists, and also their absence from positions of power in media organizations in the US as well as in European countries. The chapter has maintained that quantitative increases as such will not lead to the empowerment of professional journalists who are not male or white. This is due to the fact that gender and race are socially constructed and media organizations – just like all other organizations – are not neutral in this respect. Professional journalistic values and practices can in themselves act as tools of marginalization so employing staff from a variety of backgrounds does not necessarily lead to greater equality and diversity within the newsroom. Values that guide journalists' work are not only professional ideal typical ones but also social and cultural constructs and media organizations need to take this into account when attempting to connect better to their increasingly diverse audiences.

6 Diverse Societies, Diverse Contents

The show that saved the sitcom. And also the NBC network. The first all-Black program that avoided racial stereotyping. The top-rated show of the 1980s and the most-watched sitcom in television history. These accolades all describe *The Cosby Show* that was broadcast on the US television network NBC between 1984 and 1992, featuring the Huxtables – an upper middle class African-American family (with a medical doctor father and a lawyer mother). The sitcom has also been critically acclaimed and won a number of awards – among the most prestigious industry ones we find three Golden Globes and six Emmy Awards. The show also received a Peabody Award (an award that puts special emphasis on public service) as well as Viewers for Quality Television Awards (handed out by a non-profit organization that no longer exists which aimed to save quality shows from cancellation once their ratings dropped). However, *The Cosby Show* has been the subject of criticism as well – it was said to 'set back race relations because its view of Black assimilation fails to take into account the context of the world outside of the four walls of the Huxtable household and because it allows Whites to excuse institutional discrimination and to become desensitized to racial inequality' (Inniss and Feagin, 1995, p. 692; cf. Hopkins, 2012). *The Cosby Show* and the debates that it prompted (in industry circles, among academics as well as among policy makers) highlight issues that continue to be relevant in discussions of media representations of diverse societies.

As already suggested when applying the diversity principle to actual media systems and contents, the expectation is that media contents will reflect the predominant differences of culture, opinion and social conditions of the society at large. Also, the media are supposed to offer relevant choices of content, as well as a variety of contents over time that correspond to the needs and interests of their audiences. This means that – similarly to the case of media producers – the quantity

123

of contents devoted to various groups and issues of interest to them is not the only relevant matter, although policy makers may too often choose to go down the quantitative road. We should not only concern ourselves with how often various groups in society and their views are represented but also how they are represented and what influences such representations. Furthermore, *The Cosby Show* is an example of an entertainment programme, and the above-mentioned evaluations of this sitcom are in line with the argument – discussed in Chapter 1 in relation to larger normative theories of the media – that entertainment programmes also fulfil democratic roles. *The Cosby Show* – as already highlighted in the examples from debates that surrounded it – not only provided a space for exploring social values, it also addressed African-American social identity and it certainly created an alternative framework which drove public debate. These nuanced understandings of media contents and their roles in contemporary societies contrast with initial concerns about the influence (or indeed appeal) of media contents to audiences. The somewhat crude assumptions about the potentially corrupting influence/appeal of media contents in the 1940s and 1950s that were expressed against the backdrop of growing advertising and propaganda gave rise to models of media effects, including the hypodermic one which assumed that media contents worked like inoculations that are absorbed by the body. (For a critical history of television audience research see for example Morley, 1992; see also Moores, 1993 and Alasuutari, 1999.) The relationship between media messages and reality is not straightforward. It may seem more relevant in the case of news and current affairs and hence our expectations and indeed policy interventions are rather specific in this respect, an issue to which I return later in the chapter.

We should, however, remember another aspect of this relationship that featured in the criticisms of *The Cosby Show* – media contents do not merely reflect reality, they also construct it. Sociologically informed studies of the media have focussed on how framing – a theoretical concept that is used to uncover media's selective emphasis on certain aspects of events and issues while omitting others – shapes our social world (for an exhaustive overview of various aspects of framing see Reese et al., 2001). I mentioned in the early chapters of this book that media policies intended to support diversity by reflecting major differences in societies target contents specifically, and they can also target the media system itself. Chapter 3 discussed policy makers' efforts at preventing concentration in media markets because it can reduce the variety of players in a market and as a consequence limits the range of contents and media products available to audiences with diverse tastes and needs. This chapter opens with a consideration of why and how democratic societies regulate media contents. It makes it clear early on that ensuring effective communication – which is closely linked to the normative ideal of free speech – is particularly relevant when discussing the regulation of media contents. Public service broadcasters tend to be subjected to distinct regulatory regimes due to the very specific societal roles that they are endowed with. Commercial media – and entertainment contents in particular – are not as readily associated with socially (as opposed to economically) beneficial regulatory goals. However, I consider examples of new media technology-enabled players in the market and their possible contribution to an increased diversity of contents.

Why and how democracies regulate media contents

In May 2015 the UK newspaper *The Guardian* broke an exclusive story revealing that the Home Secretary proposed to give Ofcom new powers as part of anti-extremism measures. These would enable Ofcom – the UK's communications regulator – to take pre-emptive action against programmes that could include extremist content. According to leaked documents the then Secretary of Culture Sajid Javid opposed the move as it would put Ofcom '"into the role of a censor". It would involve "a fundamental shift in the way UK broadcasting is regulated", moving away from the current framework of post-transmission regulation which takes account of freedom of expression' (Travis, 2015). The revelation was quickly picked up by other media and sparked a wave of condemnation from organizations opposed to censorship. Not long after the publication of the leaked letter, the Queen's speech to Parliament outlined the government's proposed legislation for its new term in office which included the Extremism Bill, incorporating proposals to strengthen Ofcom's powers to take action against channels that transmit extremist content. At the time of writing (October 2015) it was unclear whether the measures would include the originally proposed pre-emptive powers but the discussions surrounding Theresa May's proposal illustrate why 'content is by far the most contentious area of media policy but it is also, in theory, the least exposed to conscious public policy actions' (Freedman, 2008, p. 122).

Liberal democratic governments are reluctant to use content regulation as a tool – as shown in Chapters 2 and 3 – mainly because 'just as censorship is seen as one of the hallmarks of authoritarian regimes, non-intervention into the minutiae of daily decisions of what to publish or broadcast is seen as a defining characteristic of pluralist government that facilitates – as long as it is legal – the distribution of both popular and unpopular, mainstream and marginal, compliant and critical ideas' (ibid., p. 122). Freedman goes on to argue that although this applies in principle, it 'bears little relation to reality, where media content is subject to a barrage of both formal and informal pressure from governments, judges, political parties, pressure groups and corporations, all of them seeking to maximize the amount of material to which they are sympathetic and minimize material which they consider damaging' (ibid., p. 122). When regulating contents – as in the case of Theresa May's proposal – commitments to freedom of speech and expression compete with the government's responsibility to protect the public interest. There is also a range of general laws that apply to media, which relate to areas such as defamation, data protection, copyright, decency and so on. We should also remember that regulation does not merely involve forbidding certain types of content, rather as suggested in previous chapters there is a range of possible policy interventions, including those aimed at the inclusion of particular socially beneficial contents (for example, Chapter 3 discussed the example of the now-dismantled Fairness Doctrine in the US). According to Baker (2002) there are three policy responses that relate to positive and negative externalities linked to media. (A positive externality is, for example, a well-informed public; a negative one is a message's impact on someone who did not want the attention, see Chapter 3 for more detail.) These policy responses are: subsidies that encourage the production of desirable contents that are not promoted by competition alone; structural interventions – ownership rules that aim to prevent concentration, for example; and the restriction of undesirable content. Baker outlines the complexity of each of these policy responses and when it comes to the suppression of 'bad' contents,

> It is disquieting that the more popular policy route, the easier approach for the political entrepreneur, is to focus on (purportedly) objectionable material and respond with calls for suppression. Positive alternatives often involve greater programmatic complexity. Promoting them requires greater, and more difficult, explanatory effort. Implementation often requires overt expenditures of resources that come from taxpayers.
>
> (ibid., p. 119)

In the following I focus on some of these policy instruments in relation to broadcasting. In many liberal democracies broadcasting is governed by statutory regulation while the press is self-regulated. The move towards self-regulation has been linked to marketization and deregulation (see Chapter 3 for more detail) so I consider some of the issues at stake here.

> Modern self-regulation ... started in the US with industry associations that defined their own code of conduct. ... The first organizations that followed these procedures were associations of newspaper publishers and editors in the 1920s. The best known fields for this type of self-regulation in Europe are the press councils that may be found in a majority of EU member countries today. The press council movement started in the 1950s in Britain and later in Germany. The first step was usually taken by the State, which planned to intervene in the matters of the industry with a law. The press industry retaliated by offering to build an autonomous structure for complaints that would be handled before independent bodies, constituted and financed by them.
>
> (Kleinsteuber, 2004, p. 64)

Self-regulatory authorities are usually set up by the industry itself, however, their establishment can be supervised by a government body. The reasons for setting up self-regulatory codes include: provision of an alternative to direct statutory regulation; prevention of direct statutory regulation by the state; building public trust/consumer confidence; avoiding legal or user-perceived liability; protecting children and other consumers; exerting moral pressure on those who would otherwise behave 'unprofessionally'; reinforcing the competitive advantage of a group of industry players; marking professional status; and raising the public image of the given industry (PCMLP, 2004). In relation to broadcasting, self-regulation is most evident in the case of public service broadcasters who establish internal bodies to self-regulate and self-monitor themselves. However, in Europe we also find examples of self-regulatory bodies that deal with commercial broadcasters. For example, in Germany the protection of minors in the media is based on the principle of co-regulation – self-regulation by Freiwillige Selbstkontrolle Fernsehen (Voluntary Television Review Body, see www.fsf.de) and the supervisory authority, the Commission for the Protection of Minors in the Media (Kommission für Jugendmedienschutz: KJM). Questions arise in relation to the accountability, transparency and efficiency of self-regulatory bodies, including the extent to which the interests of the industry overlap with the interests of consumers – that is, citizens to whom the self-regulatory bodies are accountable.

> Most attention to self-regulation and its accreditation by statutory bodies or government departments has focused on the issues of effectiveness, transparency and sanctions, i.e. with features of the self-regulatory institution and code. These aspects of the self-regulatory regime remain very relevant, but accreditation must also involve other dimensions such as financial sustainability, implications for speech freedoms and the structure of interests of the industry sector.
>
> (PCMLP, 2004, p. 86)

The shortcomings of the self-regulatory model have been discussed widely in the UK, most extensively in the context of reforms following the Leveson Inquiry into the culture, practice and ethics of the press which was launched in 2011 (see for example Petley, 2012) and recommended the creation of a new press standard body by the industry which would be backed by legislation. Debates ensued about whether Lord Justice Leveson's recommendations amounted to statutory regulation of the press, something that he firmly denied. However, this has not been the first time calls for the statutory regulation of the press were voiced in the UK. Similar arguments were raised in the early 1990s following the report of the Calcutt Committee on the self-regulatory Press Council which led to the establishment of the Press Complaints Commission (PCC). Chris Frost (2004) analyzed the complaints handled by the PCC during the first ten years of its existence to investigate whether the commission worked effectively in obliging newspapers to behave more responsibly. (The PCC claimed that it had achieved this goal.) The fact that the PCC received more than 20,000 complaints in those ten years, adjudicated only 707 and upheld 321 of them is telling. However, Frost was not interested only in statistics, rather he looked at the various areas that the complaints related to and showed that the PCC's record was particularly poor in regulating complaints about discrimination. During the ten years that Frost analyzed only six such complaints were upheld, partly because, according to the PCC code, only those named in an article could complain. (The exclusion of third parties was criticized even by the UK Culture, Media and Sport Select Committee, see House of Commons, 2015.)

Public service broadcasting – positive requirements

The principles of public service broadcasting were discussed in Chapter 2. It has also become clear from the various threads running through this book that public service broadcasting is closely associated with normative ideals, including the facilitation of a public sphere. In policies related to public service media we find diversity-oriented goals and also those linked to positive externalities associated with the media. The independence of public service broadcasters from government is crucial and one way of ensuring it is a regulatory regime that applies only to public service broadcasters and is overseen by independent supervisory bodies that represent different interests in society. There are various systems in place in European countries and they can involve self-regulatory measures.

> In terms specifically of standards in British public service broadcasting, the key mechanism employed has been the insertion of positive programme requirements into broadcasting licences. In addition to considering programming proposals in the process of franchise allocation and general statutory requirements regarding political impartiality and balance ... [the broadcasters are obligated to] provide for example, original programmes, children's programmes, religious programmes.
>
> (Feintuck and Varney, 2006, p. 70)

The public purposes of the BBC are defined in the Royal Charter as follows:

> (a) sustaining citizenship and civil society; (b) promoting education and learning; (c) stimulating creativity and cultural excellence; (d) representing the UK, its nations, regions and communities; (e) bringing the UK to the world and the world to the UK; (f) in promoting its other purposes, helping to deliver to the public the benefit of emerging communications technologies and services and, in addition, taking a leading role in the switchover to digital television.
>
> (BBC, 2015)

These public purposes are then translated into purpose remits within the Broadcasting Agreement which 'must – (a) set out priorities, and (b) specify how the BBC's performance against them will be judged, in relation to how the BBC promotes its Public Purposes in accordance with article 5 of the Charter (the BBC's mission to inform, educate and entertain)' (ibid.). For example, the public purpose of sustaining citizenship and civil society is divided into five priorities:

- Provide independent journalism of the highest quality.
- Engage a wide audience in news, current affairs and other topical issues.
- Encourage conversation and debate about news, current affairs and topical issues.
- Build greater understanding of the parliamentary process and political institutions governing the UK.
- Enable audiences to access, understand and interact with different types of media. (BBC, 2015a)

Each priority is mapped onto strategies for delivery, for example, one of those for delivering the first priority – providing independent journalism of the highest quality – states that:

> All BBC journalism will display the core values of independence, truth and accuracy, impartiality, fairness, and diversity of opinion. The BBC will maintain the strong reputation of its journalism across its portfolio of services and range of output. The quality and distinctiveness of BBC journalism will lie in its ambition to offer a broad, varied, serious and analytical news agenda with strong coverage of the UK, the nations and the English regions, and the rest of the world.
>
> (ibid.)

The actual delivery of programmes linked to the BBC's public purposes is then assessed in its annual report (for example, BBC, 2015b).

Other countries with public service broadcasting media have similar requirements to those set out in the BBC's public purposes. For example, in the case of one of the newer members of the EU, the Czech Republic, the public service broadcaster Czech Television is to serve the public by producing and broadcasting programmes accessible in the whole territory of the Czech Republic, by providing objective, verified, balanced and varied information that would help the formation of opinions, by developing the culture of the Czech nation and national and ethnic minorities, by mediating ecological information, by helping the education and upbringing of the young generation, and by contributing to viewers' entertainment (as defined in the

Act of the Czech National Council on the Czech Television No.483/1991 Coll.). We can see that the focus on minorities is clearly spelt out in the document because of the nature of public service broadcasting systems which are characterized by a high degree of internal diversity 'according to which all tastes are catered for by channels serving large, heterogeneous audiences' as opposed to 'an *"external"* and *exclusive* diversity in which different "voices" and outlooks have their own separate channels' (McQuail, 1992, p.101, original emphasis). The principle of internal diversity also applies to the UK public service broadcasting system while the Dutch one, to which McQuail was referring, is based on the principle of allocating access to associations with different outlooks and priorities. According to Dutch law, '[a] broadcasting association should aim, as laid down in its statutes, to represent some clearly stated societal, cultural, religious or philosophical stream and to direct itself in its programming to the satisfaction of some actively present social, cultural, religious or philosophical needs' (ibid., p. 100), while the actual 'allocation of broadcasting time was based on the number of members and/or subscribers to the broadcasting magazines produced by the different organizations' (Brants and McQuail, 1997, p. 155).

Impartial and balanced news

The importance of accurate and impartial news has been widely recognized as quintessential for the democratic life of societies and media policy makers have introduced safeguards that aim to ensure these. For example, in the UK the communications regulator Ofcom sets out rules in its Broadcasting Code that all commercial television and radio broadcasters must follow, including ones on due accuracy and due impartiality in news (Ofcom, 2015a). Public service broadcasters – as suggested in the description of their remit – tend to have special responsibilities where news and current affairs are concerned. These can relate to impartiality and balance in news, and in some countries we find specific requirements as to how broadly such news should be available, including that intended for children. For example, in the UK the children's channel CBBC carries the only bespoke news service for children (Newsround). Public service broadcasters tend to develop their own guidelines relating to impartiality and these are closely linked to the societal roles that they are – legally – obliged to fulfil, mostly in relation to impartial and reliable news (this, however, does not mean that public service broadcasters are not accountable to the public in this respect). The BBC's guidelines have been included in policy discussions about the transformation of state broadcasters into public service ones after the fall of communism in some countries of the former Soviet Bloc. However, the Eastern Europeans intended to implant the British model under a particular set of circumstances that were very different from the UK situation.

> The [British] broadcasters who made up this duopoly ... were serious because they could afford to be, as they did not compete for revenue. They were impartial because they were obliged to be by regulation. They were able to be impartial because they existed in a political environment in which government intervention in broadcasting was a relative rarity. ... Manifestly, neither of these sets of conditions exists in the former communist countries. ... Given these circumstances, it is naïve in the extreme to imagine that the media systems of post-communist countries can be assimilated to those of the Anglo-Saxon model.
>
> (Sparks, 1998, p. 177)

The importance of regulation aiming at the inclusion of controversial subjects and the coverage of a variety of opinions and views that may be controversial has been discussed in relation to the US Fairness Doctrine in Chapter 3. The coverage of controversial topics is also related to diversity defined as the representation of a wide range of opinions and interests that characterize society and as the provision of a channel of communication for diverse groups within society. It is thus interesting to explore how the BBC's Editorial Guidelines understand impartiality in the coverage of controversial issues.

In determining whether subjects are controversial, we should take account of:

- the level of public and political contention and debate
- how topical the subjects are
- sensitivity in terms of relevant audiences' beliefs and culture
- whether the subjects are matters of intense debate or importance in a particular nation, region or discrete area likely to comprise at least a significant part of the audience
- a reasonable view on whether the subjects are serious

- the distinction between matters grounded in fact and those which are a matter of opinion.

...

When dealing with 'controversial subjects', we must ensure a wide range of significant views and perspectives are given due weight and prominence, particularly when the controversy is active. Opinion should be clearly distinguished from fact.

(BBC, 2015c)

We can see that the BBC's guidelines reflect the ways in which diversity has been understood as a regulatory rationale in media policy. There is, however, another issue when it comes to political diversity which is linked to the provision of impartial and balanced news, and that is government interventions, which, as already suggested, were rather blunt and visible in the new democracies of 1990s Eastern Europe. I am, however, not trying to argue that political pressures on public service broadcasting are non-existent in much longer established democracies (on the UK case see Chapter 7 in Freedman, 2008). Countries such as the Czech Republic, Poland and Hungary have been building democracy since the fall of communism in 1989 and, as part of the process, they attempted to reform state broadcasters (which were under the control of the Communist Party and served as its loudspeakers) into public service ones following the British model. The major problem faced by the nascent public service broadcasting systems was the influence that politicians exercised over them. This influence was not necessarily direct, rather, bodies regulating and supervising broadcasting were dominated by politicians.

Public service broadcasting, where it has been nominally created, is usually 'parliamentary broadcasting': the role of parliament in appointing broadcasting regulatory and supervisory bodies is so strong that 'public' broadcasters do not really represent the public, but the parliamentary majority. ... In any case, public service broadcasting can hardly develop fully where civil society is weak, politicians are pre-eminent in public life and any notion of the public interest and public service is overshadowed by political interest.

(Jakubowicz, 1999, p. 57)

In Hungary, for example, political interventions in the media were characterized as a media war: 'a bitter dispute along party lines over the degree of government presence in Hungarian broadcasting that ended in a legislative debacle' (Molnar, 1999, p. 91).

> From late 1991 until 1994, the governing coalition conservative parties, overcome by their frustration with criticism, used unconstitutional tactics against the presidents of MTV [Hungarian public service television channel] and MR [Hungarian public service radio station], such as revalidating a communist government order from 1974 prescribing government control of public broadcasting – deemed unconstitutional by the constitutional Court in 1992 but upheld until the media law was passed in 1995.
>
> (ibid., p. 93)

Despite the progress with democratization (eight of the post-communist countries joined the EU in 2004), we find instances of politicians' attempts to interfere in the news production of public service broadcasters. For example, in December 2000 and January 2001, a crisis ensued at the public service Czech Television following political pressures that resulted in changes of staff (including the dismissal of Czech Television's director general). A public initiative called Czech Television – a Public Matter was launched and demonstrations were held all over the country with the aim of preventing political intervention in the running of Czech Television (for more detail see Metykova, 2005, p. 90). The problem resurfaced in October 2013 when 23 news and current affairs staff at Czech Television circulated an open letter and formally complained to the television's supervisory body about bias in news and current affairs. They argued that certain political currents benefited from coverage because of internal interference in news and current affairs (Prague Post, 2013).

Ensuring balance in media coverage becomes a much discussed topic during election campaigns and this is another area guided by regulation. Political advertising during election campaigns is strictly regulated in many democratic societies. For example, in the UK there has been a long standing ban on advertisements of a political nature on television or radio because these could give an advantage to the candidates or parties with the most significant financial resources. Instead, free airtime is provided to qualifying political parties prior to elections and Ofcom is tasked with preparing rules on their allocation, length and frequency (Ofcom, 2015b). The selection of political parties that participate in televised election debates in parliamentary democracies is also often regulated. For example, in Canada, which has been holding such debates since 1968:

> It is broadly agreed that parties need to fulfil two criteria to participate in televised debates:
>
> - They need to have representation in the House of Commons.
> - They should consistently be polling above 5 per cent in national opinion polls.
>
> An additional entry requirement is that the party leader must also be recognized as a national political figure.
>
> (Anstead, 2015, p. 9)

The UK is a relative newcomer in televised election debates and in the 2015 General Election the decision on which parties should be included in which debates remained an editorial one, with a statement on party election broadcasts stating that 'Ofcom does not determine the structure, format or timing of any possible TV leaders' election debates. The decisions on which leaders are represented in any broadcast debates are editorial matters for broadcasters in agreement with the political parties taking part' (Ofcom, 2015c). In the UK the lack of regulatory clarity combined with party fragmentation across the whole political spectrum led to lengthy discussions about which parties should be included in the debates broadcast by the BBC.

The regulatory requirement for impartial and balanced news for commercial media as well as for public service broadcasters has already been mentioned. It has also been suggested that public service broadcasters tend to have their own policies and guidelines in relation to impartiality and balance in their news coverage. They also tend to be scrutinized widely for biases in their coverage, by policy makers and activists as well as scholars. A quick search in an electronic database of academic articles uncovered as many as 474 that included the key words 'BBC impartiality'. It would be a gigantic task to try and assess whether the BBC's news coverage is impartial, under which circumstances, on which issues. However, even this brief account should make it clear that the expectation to provide impartial and balanced news is associated with public service broadcasters to a much greater extent than with commercial ones, and that the regulatory interventions for public service and commercial broadcasters differ significantly in the UK. In their analysis of the coverage of political devolution in the UK, Stephen Cushion, Justin Lewis and Gordon Ramsay explored the efficiency of editorial interventions by the BBC Trust as opposed to Ofcom's 'light touch' regulation of commercial broadcasters. They acknowledge the limitations of a single case study and conclude:

> Nonetheless, our content analysis does suggest clear and, in some cases, striking improvements after the BBC Trust's recommendations, with coverage that better reflects the new realities of devolved politics across the UK. Our case study can thus be seen to challenge claims that a 'light touch' approach is the most effective means of policing the media market in an increasingly deregulated environment. We have shown how a regulator with a public mandate for intervention can help reshape an area of journalism where coverage has lagged behind the realities of political developments in the UK. Far from regulation being a democratic obstruction on journalistic freedom, this regulatory intervention demonstrated the impact it can have on improving the accuracy of political reporting and addressing UK network failures in covering the four nations.
>
> (2012, p. 844)

In October 2014 as part of their policy goal of political diversity the UK Government commissioned Ofcom to develop a measurement framework for media plurality. Possible changes in the way contents are regulated have been proposed as a result of this consultation. The documents that had been made public by October 2015 suggest that measurement indicators will include media ownership and that they will focus on news and current affairs broadcasting. While news and current affairs are clearly linked to the information needs of citizens (and indeed to the deliberation that is key for democracy), this approach ignores the cultural dimension of media production and contents.

The news coverage of election campaigns understandably provides a lot of material for uncovering biases and hence evaluating the performance of media in this respect. This is another area that has been explored widely in policy circles, by activists as well as scholars. A report by the Loughborough University Communication Research Centre on the 2015 UK General Election found that in TV coverage (in six news programmes broadcast on different channels) the Conservative Party had the most direct quotation time overall, and that the studied newspapers (four broadsheets, five tabloids and a free paper) tended to cover the Conservative Party positively and the Labour Party negatively. It also found that the coverage in all the studied media devoted very little attention to some significant issues of public concern such as education, environment or rural affairs (for more detail see Loughborough University, 2015).

However, the questions of whether and how media manipulate on behalf of an established powerful group in society (be it a class, race or gender one) go beyond political ideological allegiances and news coverage as such, a point that I develop below. It would be difficult to argue that the coverage of minority groups (in all respects, not only in terms of representing political parties or political views that are representative of them) in news is accurate and impartial on all occasions. On the contrary, we find evidence of whole groups of citizens living in contemporary democracies being misrepresented or stereotyped. For example, there is a growing body of literature that provides nuanced analyses of news representations of Muslims in the UK, see for example Poole, 2002; Baker et al., 2013. It is true that there are ways in which media policy makers, media organizations or non-governmental organizations attempt to improve the representations of these groups, for example by increasing the number of journalists of minority backgrounds (as suggested in the previous chapter) or by training journalists in how adhering to the professional values of objectivity and impartiality does not necessarily prevent sterotypization. This is illustrated in the case of the European Roma Information Office – an international advocacy group – that devises 'ways to sensitise journalists to Roma culture in order to overcome media negative stereotyping while discussing the role of the media in combating anti-Gypsyism' (ERIO, 2015). I have shown already that there are campaigns – for example, in the UK the one fronted by Lenny Henry calling for a greater variety of measures to ensure that actors of minority ethnic backgrounds are better represented in the cultural industries – that advocate more substantial interventions by governments. It is, however, clear that the response to these calls needs to go beyond measures that support minority media ownership because these are not necessarily the most efficient in addressing diversity issues. In the case of the US Perlman argues that:

> minority ownership of broadcasting stations does influence the amount of, and content within, public affairs and news programming; not only do these stations tend to air more programs dedicated to local issues but their emphasis and choice of stories reflects stations' recognition that people of color constitute a meaningful part of the broadcasting public. In contrast, ... [a] study of cable network BET suggests that black ownership does not

necessarily yield a greater array of perspectives and, operating under the same commercial logics as other networks, produces audiences for sponsors by recycling and aping content found in other outlets. Furthermore, the constitution of the category 'minority' within broadcasting policy not only reifies white audiences as the general 'public' that broadcasters are obligated to serve but propels the fiction of a unitary minority community.

(2012, pp. 368–9)

Diversity and entertainment contents

This section considers policy interventions (or their lack) and their influence on the diversity of entertainment contents. First of all, in the 2010s the emergence of new players on the content streaming market has been welcomed as a move towards a greater diversity of contents and a broader range of representations. *The New Yorker*'s television critic Emily Nussbaum wrote the following about the series *Orange is the New Black*:

> Last year, when the women's-prison series *Orange is the New Black* débuted, on Netflix, it felt like a blast of raw oxygen. Part of this was baldly algorithmic: here, at last, were all those missing brown faces, black faces, wrinkled faces, butch lesbians, a transgender character played by a transgender actor, an ensemble of electrifying strangers, all of them so good that it seemed as if some hidden valve had been tapped, releasing fresh stories and new talent.
>
> (2014, p. 90)

Netflix also released another series dealing with a similarly unusual set-up: *Unbreakable Kimmy Schmidt* is a story of a woman who is rescued from a doomsday cult and starts life over again in New York City. The series was originally pitched to the cable network NBC but it was turned down. The competition on the television market, however, has not only led to Netflix turning to stories that would normally not be thought attractive for mainstream consumption, established cable networks have also responded to the newly arisen competitive pressures. For example, ABC launched the series *Fresh off the Boat* that depicts an Asian American family and it actually launched 20 years after the cancellation of *All-American Girl*, the last sitcom focussing on Asian Americans. These developments reflect the changes occurring in the media industries and also the greater diversification of societies, although they do not necessarily indicate a radical shift in the way media companies approach diversity and its representation in entertainment contents.

As suggested in various chapters of this book, public service broadcasters have been specifically tasked with representing diverse societies in their fictional programming with multicultural policies arguably aiming at more balanced representations of actual lived (super)diversity. While this has been the norm in Western Europe, public service broadcasters outside Europe have also produced notable popular entertainment programmes that deal with issues of diversity. One such example concerns the Canadian series *Little Mosque on the Prairie* produced by the Canadian Broadcasting Corporation and broadcast between 2007 and 2012. 'The show was notable because it was a popular success (Canada has had few successful scripted comedies) and because it deftly raised issues of religion, especially Islam, in post-9/11 North America' (Conway, 2014, p. 648). The series was noted for a number of achievements:

> One of the major challenges Muslims seem to struggle with is the construction of a space of their own, one that is flexible enough to allow the practice of their beliefs, while also making possible a degree of integration. The representations of identity and community in *Little Mosque* operate as counter-hegemonic symbolic acts that seek to illustrate the divergences and fissures that permeate the process of building a community.
>
> (Cañas 2008, p. 207)

Conway unravels the complex production decisions and circumstances that led to the making of the series when she argues that multiculturalism policies as such do not necessarily guarantee the making of this type of programming.

> First, there was the influence of topicality on content: the creator's and producers' desire to address politics within the Canadian Muslim community and prejudice against Muslims outside of it led them to create a diverse slate of characters and a setting that gave writers room to explore themes that helped viewers understand Islam better. Second, there was the influence of the content on the network-approval process, and funding and scheduling strategies.

The CBC's multicultural and regional mandates provided an impetus for the network to greenlight the show. At the same time, the show's regionalism appealed to provincial film corporations, although they were focused more on supporting their media industries than encouraging a certain type of cultural production. And the fact that *Little Mosque* was Canadian gave the CBC an advantage over its competitors during the writers guild strike. This level of institutional support in turn allowed the show's executive producers more confidence to invest their own money in the show and more leeway to explore themes that had not been explored before.

(Conway, 2014, p. 660)

However, despite increasing recognition of forms of social and cultural difference, issues relating to stereotypical representations as well as the absence/invisibility of some groups in society from mainstream entertainment contents persist. Hesmondhalgh (2013) argues that one way of explaining this phenomenon is that there are four problems that co-exist in the same genres/same texts:

1. A continuing lack of visibility or audibility, in certain genres at least ... of interesting rounded disabled characters in contemporary Hollywood and Indian films for example. 2. A continuing use of negative stereotypes and problematic representations of relatively powerless groups. ... 3. [In addition, we face] a more complex 'post-feminism' and 'post civil rights' set of representations that seemingly value the (partial) freedoms and equalities achieved by political projects such as feminism, anti-racism and socialism, but which also distance themselves from them. ... 4. [Furthermore] well-meaning and explicitly politically motivated producers, aiming to challenging [sic] existing power relations, can find themselves reproducing problematic stereotypes.

(pp. 381–2)

Hesmondhalgh's final point requires some elaboration. The unintended consequences – reproducing problematic stereotypes – have been noted by a number of scholars. Cottle, for example, argues that the occurrence of new subtle forms of racism 'is interpreted as the unintentional outcome of news producers who seek to move beyond "old fashioned racism" by portraying African Americans in more positive ways but who thereby create an impression of black social advance and thus undermine black claims on white resources and sympathies'

(Cottle, 2000, p. 11). Sarita Malik has extensively analyzed the media representations of British Asians and she argues in relation to *Grewals* – a documentary series produced by the UK-based Channel 4 which has a public service remit – that it builds on convivial culture.

> One of the characteristics of convivial culture, according to Gilroy [2004] ... is that it is also importantly a kind of culture that positions itself as racism free. Through the documentary's stylistic conventions, *The Grewals* gives an impression of truth, unmediation, and actuality cast to be representative of the *real* lived diversity out there; a typical Indian, working-class family. It comes as some relief then that they never talk about structural inequalities or social issues of race that occur outside of the Indian community, thus helping produce a sense of postracial catharsis because they symbolize an unproblematic and thriving cultural pluralism and, indeed, a depoliticized multiculturalism.
>
> (2012, pp. 524–5)

This type of programming is linked to the larger policy shift from multiculturalism policies to diversity ones – as discussed in Chapter 1 – which has contributed to the de-ethnicization of difference.

> The shift in these guiding principles is not just toward questions of recruitment practice and human resources (i.e., talent, training, mentoring, and development) but also away from the more contested, ideological terrain of cultural representation. Implicit is that more diverse recruitment and creative workers will make the difference for the equality agenda which, one presumes, also has to include questions of content. This turn away from questions of representation and identity politics is the critical dimension of this story of the rise of creative industries policy (and the shift away from multiculturalism and cultural industries policy).
>
> (Malik, 2013, p. 235)

While agreeing with the consequences of the shift from multiculturalism to integration policies, Anamik Saha argues that the wider neo-liberal environment has a serious impact on production processes.

> The seemingly positive integration of minorities into mainstream programming merely leads to further repetition of ethnic and racial stereotype, as black and Asian cultural producers, as well as

their white counterparts, are exposed to commercial forces that see exotica as a 'key competitive advantage in an overcrowded market' [Huq, 2003]. ... In this hyper-competitive climate, the BBC and Channel 4 are no longer buffered from market forces and can no longer afford to produce the kind of programmes that are beyond the reach of the commercial sector with serious ramifications for minority producers.

(2012, p. 436)

New media technologies – everyone a content maker?

The final section of this chapter considers key arguments about the proliferation of contents and content makers that is enabled by new media technologies. Apart from their role in empowering various groups in society to access and participate in communication, online media have also been discussed in relation to the production and distribution of more diverse contents than those accessible in mainstream offline media. A variety of studies have focussed on online news and current affairs, and have explored whether these follow similar trends to offline news. In their study of online news Redden and Witschge (2009) argue that mainstream online news show little diversity (one of the reasons for this could be that they are produced by transnational media businesses that rely on a limited range of sources and share a journalistic culture). The situation, however, seems to be rather different when it comes to online-only news producers (Humprecht and Büchel, 2013) and to news produced by citizen journalists. In her 2010 study Serena Carpenter measured the diversity of topics covered in online newspapers and by online citizen journalists 'by analyzing which news outlet provided a greater balance, or diversity, of topics for citizens. The results reflect that online citizen journalism content is slightly more diverse than online newspaper content. Online newspapers cover more state and national-level issues, which may limit the topics that can be covered' (p. 1075). The rise of citizen journalism – which can be broadly defined as web-based practices in which 'ordinary' users engage in journalistic practices (Goode, 2009) or as non-professionally produced media contents – has been viewed not only as possibly increasing the diversity of media contents but also as strengthening other democratic roles of the media.

It has been suggested that citizen journalism has led to a democratization of professional journalism with control over contents (gatekeeping) shifting to the audience. Luke Goode, for example, argues that:

In a mediascape characterized by scarcity, that is, finite numbers of news outlets which often share similar routines, primary sources and journalistic cultures, audience 'power' may be reduced to little more than blunt veto, that is, the option to disengage from news media as, indeed, increasing numbers of especially younger audiences have been doing. ... The democratic appeal of *online news* lies in the prospect of alleviating that scarcity and the additional democratic appeal of *citizen journalism*, more specifically, lies in the prospect of citizens themselves participating in the agenda-setting process.

(2009, p. 1292, original emphasis)

Magda Konieczna and Sue Robinson make a similar point about the role of non-profit news organizations which

are indeed based on the traditional model of trustee journalism, but ... also wish to re-define the relationship between journalists and citizens and erase the previous boundaries of informational authority. Not only are these journalists working to have citizens 'trust' to uncover those stories the local news organization failed to report, but they are also actively cultivating a sense of ownership over information and over the news organization itself for citizens.

(2014, p. 982)

With online news, audiences have new ways of engaging and – importantly – reflecting on news contents and news production which can lead to a better informed citizenry. Studies on how and why audiences engage with online news (leave comments, re-distribute news and so on) have taken into account the nature of these engagements (see for example Ksiazek et al., 2014), users' motivations to engage (for example Daughtery et al., 2008) and the quality of online user comments (Ziegele and Quiring, 2013) as well as the diversity of opinions expressed in online comments and in letters to the editor (McCluskey and Hmielowski, 2011). Research suggests that there is a potential for new media technologies to create alternative spaces of democratic empowerment. However, we should not forget that the realization of this potential depends on factors that I have already discussed – most importantly the digital divide in access to and use of the internet.

Conclusion

This chapter has considered diversity of contents and focussed in particular on how media contents are regulated on the basis of the political diversity rationale. Although liberal democratic governments are reluctant to be seen as intervening in media contents, there is actually a range of policy measures and regulations that apply to broadcast media in particular. The press has traditionally been self-regulated in the United States and European democracies and self-regulatory mechanisms have been discussed briefly. The chapter has argued that the provision of impartial, accurate and balanced news is regulated in the case of public service as well as commercial broadcasters. It explored in some detail the obligations of public service broadcasters in this respect because public service broadcasters are arguably more closely regulated and scrutinized when it comes to the provision of impartial news coverage than their commercial counterparts. Entertainment contents occupy a much less prominent place on the radar of policy makers, although issues of diverse representations and diversity of choice continue to be pertinent. The chapter has considered examples of television series showcasing complex – and sometimes critically acclaimed – representations of diversity. These, however, remain marginalized and the shift from policies of multiculturalism to diversity in public service broadcasting has led to post-racial de-politicized representations of ethnic difference. It should be stressed that the broader context of marketization and neo-liberalism has impacted on production processes that effectively encourage stereotypical depictions of difference that appeal to a wider audience and have a greater chance of succeeding in the market. The final section of the chapter considered arguments about the greater diversity of online contents and the proposed democratization of journalism, with professional journalists giving up some control over contents to 'ordinary' readers, listeners and viewers. This shift needs to be considered carefully because mainstream media companies tend to incorporate user-generated contents in ways that do not interfere with or question their editorial policies and professional practices. There are, of course, alternative online media that challenge some of the established professional practices, but their reach and impact is likely to be limited.

Conclusion

Media diversity is not an end in itself. This book has argued that it is a means of achieving a more inclusive, more democratic society. We live in countries of migration although some European democracies have only admitted this recently (Germany since the 2000s) and some continue to attempt to deny this fact (the EU member states that have joined since 2004 are examples in this respect). In the course of writing this book the so-called refugee crisis intensified and the debates about who 'they' are and what 'our' responsibilities and attitudes to 'them' (and exactly which of 'them') are, have been carried out in the mediated public sphere. Many of the issues raised, particularly in the course of the summer and autumn of 2015, relate directly to the concerns of this book. In addition, the media coverage itself provides ample opportunities to contemplate whether the sources and discourses dominating the mediated debates in various European countries represent the prevalent differences that characterize the given society at large. Assessments of the performance of media – particularly biases in coverage – are ongoing and it is clear that some national mediated public spheres are dominated by nationalist stances, often promoted by political elites (as documented in the cases of the Czech Republic, Hungary and Slovakia, see European Journalism Observatory, 2015; Hospodárske noviny, 2015).

We live in diverse societies which are becoming increasingly complex and in some cases arguably superdiverse – the transnational movement of people and media products is part of our everyday lived reality. Both of these phenomena have changed in the last few decades. Migrants arriving in developed countries can often claim no historical or cultural links to the societies in which they end up, and this applies to the refugees who fled the wars in Yugoslavia in the 1990s as much as to the refugees and migrants who have crossed the Mediterranean Sea since 2014. The circulation of transnational media contents has also intensified and it contributes to the unmaking of the myth of unified homogeneous national cultural identities. Although arguably media flows continue to be dominated by 'the West', the relationship between the homogenizing tendencies suggested by quantitative data on television programmes or on news flows has been questioned and issues of identity have been foregrounded by some scholars.

How do we co-exist in these diverse societies in inclusionary ways? How do we live multi-culture? I have briefly discussed the emergence of multiculturalism – a set of policies and strategies that were designed to manage the problems thrown up by diverse societies – which has its roots in fights for democratic citizenship rights. Multiculturalism as an official state policy that addresses living in multi-culture was largely driven underground in the 1990s. Politicians throughout Europe claimed that it did not work, even worse it resulted in parallel ethnic/ cultural/religious communities that do not aspire to be integrated into the mainstream. The term that politicians began to use for describing the aim to which policies in multicultural (or pluralistic) societies should aspire is social cohesion or integration. I have argued that, although in principle civic integration policies as such are not problematic, their actual implementations can be assimilationist and contrary to democratic citizenship. The shift from multiculturalism to civic integration has raised concerns about the openness of national cultures to difference. It has been argued vocally that changes in policies lead to the de-ethnicization and de-politicization of difference and encourage discourses about post-racial societies that have overcome structural inequalities. This, however, is far from the truth as suggested in sociological studies, and as demonstrated by events in 2015 – specifically the murder of a black pastor and eight of his parishioners – which prompted US President Barack Obama to comment on the fallacies of post-race discourse. These inequalities, of course, also relate to media. I have argued that we can think about diversity in relation to media in at least three ways – media should represent the diversity of voices and views that exist in society; the various groups that make up society should have access to channels of communication; and the various groups in society should have access to diverse contents that are of interest to them. All of these are linked to democratic citizenship. They have been translated into media policy in the form of rationales – or justifications – for regulatory interventions, namely effective communication, political diversity and cultural diversity.

There is, however, not one single way in which these policy objectives can be achieved. In Europe the public service tradition in broadcasting has been closely linked to democratic roles of media and to diversity. However, public service broadcasters have faced a fiscal squeeze, a crisis of legitimacy, marketization and the emergence of new media technologies, all of which led to changes in their role in promoting broadcasting in the public interest. A lack of political will to address issues facing public service broadcasters (and mainly to commit to addressing the normative ideal that public service broadcasting was meant to embody) has also been noted across Europe, and this is despite the fact that the roles that public service media play are not easily conferred onto other media. Commercial media that are largely regulated on the basis of economic justifications (market competition) are not regulated to deliver desirable social and cultural goals connected with media, and advertising-based funding models tend to reduce the supply of minority interest contents.

Throughout the book I have provided examples from Europe, and from the United States for comparative purposes. As in European countries, diversity is recognized as a desirable goal by US policy makers, but public service broadcasting has never played a significant role in its attainment. Rather, competition in the marketplace of ideas was thought to be the best guarantee of diverse opinions and importantly of the non-interference of the state. Yet, we need to keep in mind that market competition in media requires government intervention because media are particularly prone to market failure which hinders competition, so in fact the supposedly neutral and 'natural' competition is the result of government regulation. Some of the shortcomings of the market competition model have been recognized by US media regulators who acknowledge the lack of media that would cater for local news, women's and minority's interests and needs. The fact that competition in the marketplace of ideas can be dominated and some opinions can be drowned was recognized early on, and the Fairness Doctrine was introduced in the 1940s in order to ensure that broadcasters were legally obliged to cover controversial issues and represent contradictory opinions. This regulatory intervention was, however, annulled in the 1980s. It should be noted here that both in the UK and in the US the press has traditionally been self-regulated while broadcasting is subject to statutory regulation, and the public interest has been least robustly pursued in the case of the internet.

Political diversity has been a regulatory goal that policy makers have pursued in the case of public service broadcasters as well as commercial ones. I have argued that public service broadcasters are particularly tasked with the provision of impartial, accurate and balanced news and their performance in this respect is watched very closely (much more than their commercial counterparts). Liberal democratic governments tend to be cautious when it comes to interventions in media contents – unlike their authoritarian counterparts – but despite the apparent regulatory distance, there is a wide range of laws and policies that apply to contents. When thinking about the democratic roles of media, news and current affairs tend to be treated preferentially by policy makers as well as activists and academics. However, I have maintained throughout the book that entertainment also fulfils democratic roles and I have used the cases of *The Cosby Show* and *The Little Mosque on the Prairie* to suggest that we debate social and political values in entertainment programmes. Entertainment contents are not at the centre of policy makers' attention despite the fact that problems with the diversity of representations (or more precisely lack of these) continue to be pertinent.

The transnationalization of media, media policy and media audiences is a significant development that raises issues related to diversity. It is possible to continue imagining national audiences as homogeneous, but it is easy to see that this is not the reality that we live. Audiences have become more fragmented (or diversified) and their needs and interests are not necessarily readily served by national media. The easy and cheap availability of contents from migrants' countries of origin and their take-up are read by some as a sign of migrants' unwillingness to integrate into their new societies. However, research suggests that the information diet of migrants is highly varied. National policy makers may be oblivious to the transnational aspects of media production and consumption (and particularly to the complex links between identities and media consumption) because their concern is first and foremost with the national. However, the study of transnational media poses complex methodological and conceptual questions to scholars as well as policy makers. We can identify only a relatively small body of media research that attempts to avoid the pitfalls of the 'national container'.

Despite the proclaimed and empirically widely tested role of new media in empowering citizens, the digital divide continues to exist along gender, racial and income lines and even if access has improved, inequalities in use continue to exist (that is, those who are well off and well educated are more empowered by internet use). The emergence of new media technologies has not made the normative ideal of the public sphere redundant. Despite initial enthusiasm about the abundance and diversity of contents that the internet offers, studies indicate that mainstream news contents online are not more diverse than offline, and the proposed democratization of journalism resulting from professional journalists giving up some of the control over contents to 'ordinary' readers, listeners and viewers has not been as radical as suggested by some. New media technologies have introduced greater competition in streaming contents and some of the programmes have been highly commended for representing marginalized groups in society in a complex manner (such as Netflix's series *Orange is the New Black*).

Media play a wide range of roles in our lives and they are also very special cultural and economic products. It has always been the case that complex phenomena need to be addressed in complex ways and policy makers should be aware of the pitfalls of reductionism. The book has considered the position of women and members of ethnic minority groups in professional journalism. I have suggested that increasing the number of these under-represented groups in the profession is unlikely to be sufficient to address the stereotypical reporting on these groups or indeed the outright absence of coverage of issues that are of interest to them. Gender and race are socially constructed and the nature of the journalistic profession suppresses the influence of individual characteristics on news and current affairs. This does not mean that we should give up on attempting to remedy these inequalities; on the contrary, we need more complex and wider reaching policy instruments than the ones that have been promoted. Importantly, when developing policies related to media diversity, we need to take into account the larger context of deregulation and the shift from citizen-oriented to consumer-oriented policy making, and last but not least the pitfalls of post-racial discourse.

The more abstract level of policy making has been central throughout the book. Societies and their media systems do not exist in a vacuum, they are the result of explicit policies and regulations. The 'battles' around what these policies should look like are played out in the judicial and political arenas and we need to keep in mind that policy making processes can themselves become politicized. I have – at least briefly – traced some of the trends in media regulation, most notably the influence of marketization and deregulation in the sphere of media. The shift away from multiculturalism policies related to the media has been discussed at some length, particularly in relation to public service broadcasting, with scholars presenting convincing arguments and data about the detrimental impact of the shift towards integrationist policies (which in the UK involve broader conceptualizations of cultural diversity). Some of the proposed policy changes have sparked remarkable responses among 'ordinary' citizens. For example, in 2015 the net neutrality campaign in the United States triggered an unprecedented number of responses which crashed the regulator's website and the UK

Government's proposed changes to the BBC's funding and operation prompted nation-wide campaigns. However, such public scrutiny of and response to a media policy issue is rather rare.

The book has provided many examples of why media policy matters and why the existing arrangements are not necessarily supportive of the media's democratic roles, particularly within the diversity framework. So what kind of media policy and media policy making would enhance greater media diversity and – among other goals – align the 'social heterogeneity that physically exists and serves as a selection source for media, and a discursive heterogeneity on society within media content' (Raeijmaekers and Maeseele, 2015, p. 1051)?

We need to keep in mind normative ideals linked with the media's democratic roles and I have argued that Habermas' normative ideal of the public sphere continues to be relevant. However, 'questions of media structure and performance are essentially political and ideological questions that imply a dialogue or conflict between different values. Democratization of communication is not seen as a one-way street but a process of contestation' (Karppinen, 2007, p. 25). For improved media policy making above all we need to recognize and debate competing visions of society and of the public sphere. This means that we need to acknowledge that diversity and pluralism are not neutral concepts and also that we need political decisions which 'are made between real alternatives and which imply the availability of conflicting, but legitimate projects on how to organize common affairs' (ibid.).

James Curran (2002a) argues that a democratic media system should facilitate the expression of conflict and difference as well as assist social conciliation. He suggests that we should not think about media 'as a single institution with a common democratic purpose. Rather, different media should be viewed as having different functions within the democratic system, calling for different kinds of structure and styles of journalism' (p. 239). The pluralistic media design that he proposes consists of a specialist sector that enables 'different social groups to debate within their terms of reference issues of social identity, group interest, political strategy and social-moral values. Part of this sector should also aid social groups to organize effectively' (p. 240). Sitting above this specialist sector are general media that enable the society as a whole to come together and debate. Curran's model incorporates public service television at its core and four other sectors on the periphery: civic media, professional media, social market and a conventional private media sector. Such a re-modelling of the media system has thus far not found a place in policy debates because in ongoing media regulatory practice structural regulation 'refers to the limits on the extent of that which can be owned within any market by any one corporate entity' (Feintuck, 1999, p. 51) and does not involve the creation of socially desirable media outlets. I have discussed the existence of minority media and community media, with the latter being supported in government media policy. However, their introduction does not equate to a focussed attempt at re-structuring the media system in order to enable greater inclusivity. I have also suggested that despite technological advances, access to the mediated public sphere remains limited for some marginalized groups.

Encouraging the creation of media that are not based on the prevalent models of funding, organization and production practices can also indirectly contribute to increasing the numbers of women and representatives of ethnic minority groups in positions of power within media organizations. As mentioned in Chapter 5 open electoral processes can encourage more gender-equal situations in the media. However, appointments within the prevalent media hierarchies tend not to rely on electoral processes and can thus hinder the prospects of members of minority groups. In the UK discussions about the representation of black and ethnic minority professionals in the media industries also pose questions about the suitability of quotas. Compared to commercial companies, public service broadcasters, as demonstrated in the case of the BBC and the setting up of the diversity creative talent fund, are more closely scrutinized in terms of the ethnic and gender make-up of their staff and the interventions that they devise in this respect. However, increasing the number of media professionals of minority backgrounds is only one issue that media policy makers should take into account. Because gender and ethnicity are socially constructed, there is a need to address the complex issues of socialization within media organizations, an area which is normally outside the radar of policy makers. Professional training that is intended to sensitize journalists to the stereotyping of vulnerable groups in society (as discussed in the case of the Roma) can also contribute to more inclusive reporting in the media.

Media policies relate to areas that are crucial for the maintenance of minority languages and cultures, and this connection could be addressed more extensively in media policies. As societies grow more diverse and complex, the transnational aspects of media and their uses become more pronounced. However, the transnational dimension of media policy making is limited and in the case of EU member states restricted to issues of competition. Yet there are aspects of citizenship that are transnational in nature and are ignored in media policies that address the 'national container' only. I have referred to the case of the Roma, Europe's largest and arguably most marginalized minority, whose needs are marginalized at national level media policy making and absent at the pan-European level.

As I have already pointed out public service broadcasting is closely linked to the normative ideal of the public sphere. Although – as I have shown in this book – the empirical manifestations of the mediated public sphere fall short of the ideal, this is not a reason to discard public service broadcasting as a means of ensuring the media's democratic roles. Technological developments do not make public service ideals obsolete or unnecessary. On the contrary, public service media become even more relevant, as Graham Murdock argues: 'We have to stop thinking of public broadcasting as a stand-alone organization and see it as a principal node in an emerging network of public and civil initiatives that taken together provide the basis for new shared cultural space, a digital commons' (2004). In Chapter 3 I offered a range of examples and arguments that clearly demonstrate that market competition is overall an insufficient regulatory mechanism for ensuring the democratic roles of the media. Media policy makers need to acknowledge the limitations of competition as a regulatory mechanism and recognize that the quantifiable and measurable performance indicators of diversity do not take into account the qualitative and multi-faceted goals associated with media in democratic societies. Ideals – such as freedom of speech – that are linked to regulatory rationales need to be critically examined otherwise their 'mythological status' makes them susceptible to mobilization for political interests.

I cannot conclude the book without at least briefly considering the nature of professional journalism and the roles that are ascribed to it in democratic societies. Does professional journalism promote values and practices that may actually disadvantage some groups in society? I have presented the arguments in Chapter 5, and although there has been extensive research on gender and the constraints of professional journalistic values and practices, the available data are not conclusive. However, this does not mean that policy makers should refrain from exploring avenues for encouraging alternative forms of journalism which might develop with the emergence of alternative online spaces and the search for new business models and new forms of storytelling. Advocacy journalism, citizen journalism and various forms of witnessing by the public are only a few examples that arguably present avenues for empowering marginalized groups in society. Nonetheless, these groups may not be exposed to such forms of journalism, let alone be actively involved in their practice. As I mentioned in the Introduction, media diversity raises complex issues and requires complex regulatory responses, and the closer co-operation between policy makers and stakeholders in the policy making process (including civil society actors, academics and researchers) could contribute to these.

Bibliography

Aksoy, A. and Robins, K. (2003) 'The Enlargement of Meaning: Social Demand in a Transnational Context', *International Communication Gazette*, 65(4–5), 365–88.

Alasuutari, P. (1999) *Rethinking the Media Audience: The New Agenda* (London: Sage).

Alibhai-Brown, Y. (2000) *After Multiculturalism* (London: The Foreign Policy Centre).

Anderson, M. (2014) 'As News Business Takes a Hit, The Number of Black Journalists Declines', http://www.pewresearch.org/fact-tank/2014/08/01/as-news-business-takes-a-hit-the-number-of-black-journalists-declines/, date accessed 20 October 2015.

Anderson, M. (2015) A Rising Share of the U.S. Black Population Is Foreign Born (Pew Research Center: Social and Demographic Trends), http://www.pewsocialtrends.org/2015/04/09/a-rising-share-of-the-u-s-black-population-is-foreign-born/, date accessed 20 October 2015.

Anstead, N. (2015) 'Televised Debates in Parliamentary Democracies,' LSE Media Policy Brief 13, http://www.lse.ac.uk/media@lse/documents/MPP/LSE-MPP-Policy-Brief-13-Televised-Election-Debates-in-the-UK.pdf, date accessed 19 February 2016.

Appadurai, A. (1990) 'Disjuncture and Difference in the Global Cultural Economy', *Theory Culture Society*, 7, 295–310.

Arnold, A. and Schneider, B. (2007) 'Communicating Separation? Ethnic Media and Ethnic Journalists as Institutions of Integration in Germany', *Journalism*, 8(2), 115–36.

ASNE (2015) 'Minority Employment in Daily Newspapers', http://asne.org/content.asp?pl=140&sl=129&contentid=129, date accessed 20 October 2015.

ASNE (2015a) '2015 Census', http://asne.org/content.asp?pl=121&sl=415&contentid=415, date accessed 20 October 2015.

Aufderheide, P. (1996) 'Public Service Broadcasting in the United States', *Journal of Media Economics*, 9(1), 63–76.

Awad, I. (2011) 'Latinas/os and the Mainstream Press: The Exclusions of Professional Diversity', *Journalism*, 12(5), 515–32.

Awad, I. and Roth, A. (2011) 'From Minority to Cross-cultural Programmes: Dutch Media Policy and the Politics of Integration', *The International Communication Gazette*, 73(5), 400–18.

Bagdikian, B. (1997) *The Media Monopoly*, 5th edn (Boston: Beacon Press).

Bagdikian, B. (2004) *The New Media Monopoly*, 20th edn (Boston: Beacon Press).

Bailey, O., Cammaerts, B. and Carpentier, N. (2007) (eds) *Understanding Alternative Media* (Maidenhead: Open University Press).

Bakan, J. (2004) *The Corporation: The Pathological Pursuit of Profit and Power* (London: Constable & Robinson).

Baker, C.E. (2002) *Media, Markets and Democracy* (Cambridge: Cambridge University Press).

Baker, P., Gabrielatos, C. and McEnery, T. (2013) *Discourse Analysis and Media Attitudes: The Representation of Islam in the British Press* (Cambridge: Cambridge University Press).

Banks, J. (1997) 'MTV and the Globalization of Popular Culture', *International Communication Gazette*, 59(1), 43–60.

Barnett, S. (2010) 'Minding the Regional News Gap', *British Journalism Review*, 21(1), 13–18.

Barron, J.A. (1967) 'Access to the Press – A New First Amendment Right', *Harvard Law Review*, 80(8), 1641–78.

Bartram, D., Poros, M.V. and Monforte, P. (2014) *Key Concepts in Migration* (London: Sage).

BBC (2014) 'Creative Diversity Development Fund Launched', http://www.bbc .co.uk/commissioning/news/articles/creative-diversity-development-fund-launched, date accessed 26 January 2016.

BBC (2015) 'Charter and Agreement', http://www.bbc.co.uk/bbctrust/governance/ regulatory_framework/charter_agreement.html, date accessed 30 October 2015.

BBC (2015a) 'Inside the BBC', http://www.bbc.co.uk/aboutthebbc/insidethebbc/ whoweare/publicpurposes/citizenship.html, date accessed 30 October 2015.

BBC (2015b) 'Media Centre', http://www.bbc.co.uk/mediacentre/latest-news/2015/annual-report, date accessed 30 October 2015.

BBC (2015c) 'Editorial Guidelines', http://www.bbc.co.uk/editorialguidelines/ guidelines/impartiality/controversial-subjects, date accessed 30 October 2015.

Beam, M. and Kosicki, G. (2014) 'Personalized News Portals: Filtering Systems and Increased News Exposure', *Journalism and Mass Communication Quarterly*, 91(1), 59–77.

Beck, U. (2006) 'Cosmopolitan Society and Its Adversaries' in *The Cosmopolitan Vision* (Cambridge: Polity).

Ben-David, A. (2012) 'The Palestinian Diaspora on the Web: Between De-territorialization and Re-territorialization', *Social Science Information*, 51(4), 459–74.

Berte, K. and de Bens, E. (2008) 'Newspapers go for Advertising: Challenges and Opportunities in a Changing Media Environment', *Journalism Studies*, 9(5), 692–703.

Blaagaard, B. (2013) 'Shifting Boundaries: Objectivity, Citizen Journalism and Tomorrow's Journalists', *Journalism*, 14(8), 1076–90.

Blumler, J.G. (1993) 'Meshing Money with Mission: Purity versus Pragmatism in Public Broadcasting', *European Journal of Communication*, 8(4), 403–24.

Bonini, T. (2011) 'The Media as "Home-Making" Tools: Life Story of a Filipino Migrant in Milan', *Media, Culture and Society*, 33(6), 869–83.

Bourdon, J. (2007) 'Unhappy Engineers of the European Soul: The EBU and the Woes of Pan-European Television', *The International Communication Gazette*, 69(3), 263–80.

Box Office Mojo (2015) http://www.boxofficemojo.com/movies/?id=godzilla2012 .htm, date accessed 15 November 2015.

Boyd-Barrett, O. (1980) *The International News Agencies* (Edinburgh: Constable).

Boyd-Barrett, O. and Rantanen, T. (1999) *The Globalization of News* (London: Sage).

Braman, S. (2004) 'Where has Media Policy Gone? Defining the Field in the Twenty-first Century', *Communication Law and Policy*, 9(2), 153–82.

Brants, K. and McQuail, D. (1997) 'The Netherlands' in B.S. Ostergaard (ed.) *The Media in Western Europe: The Euromedia Handbook* (London: Sage).

Breen, M. (2010) 'Digital Determinism: Culture Industries in the USA-Australia Free Trade Agreement', *New Media and Society*, 12(4), 657–76.

Broersma, M. (2010) 'The Unbearable Limitations of Journalism: On Press Critique and Journalism's Claim to Truth', *The International Communication Gazette*, 72(1), 21–33.

Brown, K.S. and Cavazos, R.J. (2002) 'Network Revenues and African American Broadcast Television Programs', *Journal of Media Economics*, 15(4), 227–39.

Browne, D.E. (2005) *Ethnic Minorities, Electronic Media and the Public Sphere: A Comparative Approach* (Cresskill, NJ: Hampton Press).

Brubaker, R. (1992) *Citizenship and Nationhood in France and Germany* (Cambridge, MA: Harvard University Press).

Brubaker, R. (2001) 'The Return of Assimilation? Changing Perspectives on Immigration and its Sequels in France, Germany, and the United States', *Ethnic and Racial Studies*, 24(4), 531–48.

Brüggemann, M. and Schulz-Forberg, H. (2009) 'Becoming Pan-European? Transnational Media and the European Public Sphere', *The International Communication Gazette*, 71(8), 693–712.

Budarick, J. (2014) 'Media and the Limits of Transnational Solidarity: Unanswered Questions in the Relationship between Diaspora, Communication and Community', *Global Media and Communication*, 10(2), 139–53.

Business Dictionary (2015) 'Public Good', http://www.businessdictionary.com/ definition/public-good.html#ixzz3eB2OFn5i, date accessed 20 November 2015.

Byerly, C.M. (ed.) (2013) *The Palgrave International Handbook of Women and Journalism* (Basingstoke: Palgrave Macmillan).

Calabrese, A. (2004) 'Stealth Regulation: Moral Meltdown and Political Radicalism at the Federal Communications Commission', *New Media and Society*, 6(1), 106–13.

Calhoun, C. (ed.) (1997) *Habermas and the Public Sphere* (Cambridge, MA: Massachusetts Institute of Technology).

Cameron, D. (2011) 'PM's speech at Munich Security Conference', https://www.gov.uk/government/speeches/pms-speech-at-munich-security-conference, date accessed 10 October 2015.

Campos-Castillo, C. (2014) 'Revisiting the First-Level Digital Divide in the United States: Gender and Race/Ethnicity Patterns, 2007–2012', *Social Science Computer Review*, 1(17), 423–39.

Cañas, S. (2008) 'The Little Mosque on the Prairie: Examining (Multi) Cultural Spaces of Nation and Religion', *Cultural Dynamics*, 20(3), 195–211.

Carpenter, S. (2010) 'A Study of Content Diversity in Online Citizen Journalism and Online Newspaper Articles', *New Media & Society*, 12(7), 1064–84.

Carroll, R. (2013) 'Obama Praises "Exceptional" Hollywood at Star-studded Fundraiser', *The Guardian*, http://www.theguardian.com/world/2013/nov/26/obama-dreamworks-hollywood-fundraisers, date accessed 15 November 2015.

Census 2014 (2015) State and County Quick Facts, http://quickfacts.census.gov/qfd/states/00000.html, date accessed 20 October 2015.

Chalaby, J.K. (1996) 'Journalism as an Anglo-American Invention: A Comparison of the Development of French and Anglo-American Journalism, 1830s–1920s', *European Journal of Communication* 11(3), 303–26.

Chalaby, J.K. (2005) 'From Internationalization to Transnationalization', *Global Media and Communication*, 1(1), 28–33.

Chalaby, J.K. (2005a) (ed.) *Transnational Television Worldwide: Towards a New Media Order* (London: I.B. Tauris).

Chambers, D., Steiner, L. and Fleming, C. (2004) *Women and Journalism* (London: Routledge).

Chris, C. (2006) 'Can You Repeat That? Patterns of Media Ownership and the "Repurposing" Trend', *The Communication Review*, 9(1), 63–84.

Christiansen, C.C. (2004) 'News Media Consumption among Immigrants in Europe: The Relevance of Diaspora', *Ethnicities* 4(2), 185–207.

Cole, P. (1998) 'The Limits of Inclusion', *Soundings*, 10, 124–44.

Collins, R. (1994) *Broadcasting and Audiovisual Policy in the European Single Market* (London: Routledge).

Conlan, T. (2014) 'Lenny Henry Campaign: Back TV Diversity or We'll Boycott Licence Fee', *The Guardian*, http://www.theguardian.com/media/2014/apr/23/lenny-henry-campaign-tv-diversity-licence-fee, date accessed 15 November 2015.

Connor, P., Cohn, D. and Gonzalez-Barrera, A. (2013) *Changing Patterns of Global Migration and Remittances*. (Washington DC: Pew Research Center: Social and Demographic Trends), http://www.pewsocialtrends.org/2013/12/17/changing-patterns-of-global-migration-and-remittances, date accessed 20 October 2015.

Conway, K. (2014) '*Little Mosque*, Small Screen: Multicultural Broadcasting Policy and Muslims on Television', *Television and New Media*, 15(7), 648–663.

Cooper, M. (2003) *Media Ownership and Democracy in the Digital Information Age* (Stanford: Centre for Internet and Society, Stanford Law School).

Cottle, S. (2000) (ed.) *Ethnic Minorities and the Media* (Milton Keynes: Open University Press).

Council of Europe (1992) 'European Charter for Regional or Minority Languages', https://rm.coe.int/CoERMPublicCommonSearchServices/DisplayDCTMCont ent?documentId=090000168007bf4b, date accessed 5 October 2015.

Creative Skillset (undated), Annual Report 2013/14, http://creativeskillset.org/ assets/0001/0217/Annual_Report_2013-14.pdf, date accessed 5 October 2015.

Curran, J. (1998) 'Crisis of Public Communication: A Reappraisal' in T. Liebes and J. Curran (eds) *Media, Ritual and Identity* (London: Routledge).

Curran, J. (2002) 'Global Media Concentration: Shifting the Argument', *Open Democracy*, https://www.opendemocracy.net/media-globalmediaownership/ article_37.jsp, date accessed 20 October 2015.

Curran, J. (2002a) *Media and Power* (London: Routledge), e-book.

Curran, J. (2010) 'Democratic Value of Entertainment: A Reappraisal', *Media & Jornalismo*, 9(2), 69–87.

Cushion, S., Lewis, J. and Ramsay, G.N. (2012) 'The Impact of Interventionist Regulation in Reshaping News Agendas: A Comparative Analysis of Public and Commercially Funded Television Journalism', *Journalism*, 13(7), 831–849.

Dahlgren, P. (1991) 'Introduction' in P. Dahlgren and C. Sparks (eds) *Communication and Citizenship: Journalism and the Public Sphere in the New Media Age* (London: Routledge).

Daughtery, T., Eastin, M.S. and Bright, L. (2008) 'Exploring Consumer Motivations for Creating User-Generated Content', *Journal of Interactive Advertising*, 8(2), 16–25.

Davis, A. (2013) *Promotional Cultures: The Rise and Spread of Advertising, Public Relations, Marketing and Branding* (Cambridge: Polity).

De Bens, E. and de Smaele, H. (2001) 'The Inflow of American Television Fiction on European Broadcasting Channels Revisited', *European Journal of Communication*, 16(1), 51–76.

de Bruin, M. and Ross, K. (2004) (eds) *Gender and Newsroom Cultures: Identities at Work* (Creskill, NJ: Hampton Press).

De Varennes, F. (1996) *Language, Minorities and Human Rights* (The Hague: Kluwer Law International).

Department for Culture, Media and Sport (2014) 'Creative Industries Economic Estimates', https://www.gov.uk/government/uploads/system/uploads/ attachment_data/file/271008/Creative_Industries_Economic_Estimates_-_ January_2014.pdf, date accessed 15 November 2015.

DESTATIS (2015) '2013: Highest Level of Immigration to Germany for 20 Years', https://www.destatis.de/EN/FactsFigures/SocietyState/Population/Migration/ Current.html;jsessionid=3C928DA15C15309F25CF15D7567CA6C6.cae1, date accessed 15 November 2015.

Deuze, M. (2005) 'What is Journalism?: Professional Identity and Ideology of Journalists Reconsidered', *Journalism* 6(4), 442–64.

Dini, P., Milne, C. and Milne, R. (2012) *Costs and Benefits of Superfast Broadband in the UK* (London: LSE Enterprise), http://www.lse.ac.uk/businessAndConsultancy/ LSEConsulting/pdf/SuperfastBroadband.pdf, date accessed 19 February 2016.

Djerf-Pierre, M. (2005) 'Lonely at the Top: Gendered Media Elites in Sweden', *Journalism*, 6(3), 265–90.

Downey, J. and Fenton, N. (2003) 'New Media, Counter Publicity and the Public Sphere', *New Media and Society*, (5)2, 185–202.

Doyle, G. (2002) *Media Ownership: The Economics and Politics of Convergence and Concentration* (London: Sage).

Doyle, G. (2005) *Understanding Media Economics* (London: Sage).

Dyson, K. and Humphreys, P. (1986) 'Policies for New Media in Western Europe: Deregulation of Broadcasting and Multimedia Diversification', *West European Politics*, 9(4), 98–124.

Eckert, S. and Chadha, K. (2013) 'Muslim Bloggers in Germany: An Emerging Counterpublic', *Media, Culture and Society*, 35(8), 926–42.

Einstein, M. (2004) *Media Diversity: Economics, Ownership, and the FCC* (London: Lawrence Erlbaum Associates).

Emden, C. and Midgley, D. (2012) (eds) *Changing Perceptions of the Public Sphere* (New York: Berghahn).

Erdal, I.J. (2009) 'Repurposing of Content in Multi-Platform News Production', *Journalism Practice*, 3(2), 178–195.

ERIO (2015) 'Projects', http://www.erionet.eu/projects.htm, date accessed 30 October 2015.

Esser, F., de Vreese, C., Strömbäck, J., van Aelst, P., Aalberg, T., Stanyer, J., Lengauer, G., Berganza, R., Legnante, G., Papathanassopoulos, S., Salgado, S., Sheafer, T. and Reinemann, C. (2012) 'Political Information Opportunities in Europe: A Longitudinal and Comparative Study of Thirteen Television Systems', *The International Journal of Press/Politics*, 17(3), 247–74.

Esser, F. and Umbricht, A. (2013) 'Competing Models of Journalism? Political Affairs Coverage in U.S., British, German, Swiss, French and Italian Newspapers', National Centre of Competence in Research (NCCR) Challenges to Democracy in the 21st Century Working Paper No. 55, http://www.nccr-democracy.uzh .ch/publications/workingpaper/pdf/wp_55.pdf, date accessed 20 October 2015.

Europa (2015) 'Competition', http://ec.europa.eu/competition/consumers/why_ en.html, date accessed 30 October 2015.

Europa (2015a) *Indicators for Media Pluralism in the Member States – Towards a Risk-Based Approach*, https://ec.europa.eu/digital-agenda/sites/digital-agenda/ files/final_report_09.pdf, date accessed 27 January 2016.

Europa (2015b) 'The Media Pluralism Monitor', http://ec.europa.eu/digital- agenda/en/independent-study-indicators-media-pluralism, date accessed 15 November 2015.

European Commission (2011) 'Communication from The Commission to The European Parliament, The Council, The European Economic and Social Committee and The Committee of The Regions: An EU Framework for National Roma Integration Strategies up to 2020', http://ec.europa.eu/ justice/policies/discrimination/docs/com_2011_173_en.pdf, date accessed 20 February 2016.

European Commission (2015) European Commission – Press Release, http://europa
.eu/rapid/press-release_IP-15-4780_en.htm, date accessed 10 October 2015.

European Journalism Observatory (2015) 'Research: How Europe's Newspapers
Reported the Migration Crisis', http://en.ejo.ch/research/research-how-europes-
newspapers-reported-the-migration-crisis, date accessed 15 November 2015.

Eword, The (2015) Search Engine Market, http://theeword.co.uk/info/search_
engine_market, date accessed 10 October 2015.

Eurostat (2015) 'EU Citizenship: Statistics on Cross-border Activities', http://
ec.europa.eu/eurostat/statistics-explained/index.php/EU_citizenship_-_
statistics_on_cross-border_activities, date accessed 15 November 2015.

Fahs, A. (2011) *Out on Assignment: Newspaper Women and the Making of Modern
Public Space* (The University of North Carolina Press).

Falk, F. and Grizard, E. (2005) 'The "Glass Ceiling" Persists: Women Leaders in
Communication Companies', *Journal of Media Business Studies* 2(1), 23–49.

FCC (2015) 'Emergency Information', http://transition.fcc.gov/osp/inc-report/
INoC-17-Emergency-Information.pdf, date accessed 30 October 2015.

FCC (2015a) 'Commission Document', https://www.fcc.gov/document/
chairmans-statement-comcast-twc-merger, date accessed 30 October 2015.

FCC (2015b) 'FCC Takes Steps to Modernize and Reform Lifeline for Broadband',
https://www.fcc.gov/document/fcc-takes-steps-modernize-and-reform-life-
line-broadband, date accessed 30 October 2015.

Federal Foreign Office (2015) 'Immigration Act', http://www.auswaertiges-amt.
de/EN/EinreiseUndAufenthalt/Zuwanderungsrecht_node.html, date accessed
30 October 2015.

Feintuck, M. (1999) *Media Regulation: Public Interest and the Law* (Edinburgh:
Edinburgh University Press).

Feintuck, M. and Varney, M. (2006) *Media Regulation, Public Interest and the Law*
(Edinburgh: Edinburgh University Press).

Feldstein, M. (2006) 'A Muckraking Model: Investigative Reporting Cycles in
American History', *The Harvard International Journal of Press/Politics* 11(2), 105–20.

Fenton, N. (2010) *New Media, Old News: Journalism and Democracy in the Digital
Age* (London: Sage).

Fenton, N., Metykova, M., Schlosberg, J. and Freedman, D. (2010) *Meeting the
News Needs of Local Communities* (London: Media Trust).

Figenschou, T.U. (2014) *Al Jazeera and the Global Media Landscape: The South Is
Talking Back* (New York: Routledge).

Fisher, C. (2015) 'The Advocacy Continuum: Towards a Theory of Advocacy in
Journalism', *Journalism*, 1–16.

Foldy, E. (2012) 'Something of Collaborative Manufacture: The Construction
of Race and Gender Identities in Organizations', *The Journal of Applied
Behavioral Science* 48(4), 495–524.

Forbes (2015) Netflix Q1 Earnings: The Stock Soars As Subscriber Numbers
Impress, http://www.forbes.com/sites/greatspeculations/2015/04/17/netflix-
q1-earnings-the-stock-soars-as-subscriber-numbers-impress/, date accessed 10
October 2015.

Franklin, B. and Murphy, D. (eds) (1998) *Making the Local News: Local Journalism in Context* (London: Routledge).

Franks, S. (2013) *Women and Journalism* (London: I.B. Tauris).

Fraser, N. (1993) 'Rethinking the Public Sphere' in B. Robbins (ed.) *The Phantom Public Sphere* (Minneapolis: University of Minnesota Press).

Free Press (2015) 'Join the Fight to Stop the Comcast-Time Warner Cable Merger', http://www.freepress.net/resource/105883/join-fight-stop-comcast-time-warner-cable-merger, date accessed 30 October 2015.

Freedman, D. (2008) *The Politics of Media Policy* (Cambridge: Polity).

Frost, C. (2004) 'The Press Complaints Commission: The Study of Ten Years of Adjudications on Press Complaints', *Journalism Studies*, 5(1), 104–14.

Galtung, J. and Ruge, M. Holmboe (1965) 'The Structure of Foreign News: The Presentation of the Congo, Cuba and Cyprus Crises in Four Norwegian Newspapers', *Journal of Peace Research*, 2(1), 64–90.

Gans, H. (1979) 'Symbolic Ethnicity: The Future of Ethnic Groups and Cultures in America', *Ethnic and Racial Studies*, 2(1), 1–20.

Garnham, N. (1990) *Capitalism and Communication: Global Culture and the Economics of Information*, ed. by Fred Inglis (London: Sage).

Garnham, N. (2005) 'From Cultural to Creative Industries: An Analysis of the Implications of the "Creative Industries" Approach to Arts and Media Policy Making in the United Kingdom', *International Journal of Cultural Policy*, 11(1), 15–29.

Geissler, R. and Potker, H. (2008) *Media, Migration, Integration: The European and North American Perspective* (Rutgers: Transaction).

Georgiou, M. (2007) 'Transnational Crossroads for Media and Diaspora: Three Challenges for Research' in O. Geddes Bailey, M. Georgiou and R. Harindranath (eds) *Transnational Lives and the Media: Re-imagining Diaspora* (New York: Palgrave Macmillan).

Ghorashi, H. and Broersma, K. (2009) 'The "Iranian Diaspora" and the New Media: From Political Action to Humanitarian Help', *Development and Change*, 40(4), 667–91.

Giddens, A. (1991) *The Consequences of Modernity* (Cambridge: Polity).

Gill, R. (2007) *Gender and the Media* (Cambridge: Polity Press).

Gilroy, P. (2002) *There Ain't No Black in the Union Jack: The Cultural Politics of Race and Nation* (London: Routledge).

Gilroy, P. (2004) *After Empire: Melancholia or Convivial Culture* (London: Routledge).

Gitlin, T. (1998) 'Public Sphere or Public Sphericules?' in T. Liebes and J. Curran (eds) *Media, Ritual and Identity* (London: Routledge).

Glevarec, H. and Pinet, M. (2008) 'From Liberalization to Fragmentation: A Sociology of French Radio Audiences since the 1990s and the Consequences for Cultural Industries Theory', *Media, Culture and Society*, 30(2), 215–38.

Goode, L. (2009) 'Social News, Citizen Journalism and Democracy', *New Media and Society*, 11(8), 1287–1305.

Goodman, E.P. (2007) 'Media Policy and Free Speech: The First Amendment at War With Itself', *Hofstra Law Review*, 35, 1211–17.

Google (2013) 'Quantifying Movie Magic', http://adwords.blogspot.co.uk/2013/06/quantifying-movie-magic-with-google.html, date accessed 20 October 2015.

Graziano, T. (2012) 'The Tunisian Diaspora: Between "Digital Riots" and Web Activism', *Social Science Information*, 51(4), 534–50.

Greater London Authority (2015) 'London Datastore', http://data.london.gov.uk/dataset/london-borough-profiles, date accessed 20 October 2015.

Greater London Authority (2015a) 'London Datastore', http://data.london.gov.uk/dataset/languages-spoken-pupils-borough-msoa, date accessed 20 October 2015.

Griffin, A. (2014) 'Where are the Women?' http://niemanreports.org/articles/where-are-the-women/, date accessed 20 October 2015.

Habermas, J. (1989) *The Structural Transformation of the Public Sphere* (Cambridge, MA: MIT Press).

Haggerty, A. (2014) 'National Newspaper Industry Working on New System of Audience Measurement', *The Drum*, http://www.thedrum.com/news/2014/07/10/national-newspaper-industry-working-new-system-audience-measurement, date accessed 25 October 2015.

Hall, S. (1993) 'Which Public, Whose Service?' in W. Stevenson (ed.) *All Our Futures: The Changing Role And Purpose of the BBC* (London: The British Film Institute).

Hall, S. (2000) 'Conclusion: The Multi-cultural Question' in B. Hesse (ed.) *Un/Settled Multiculturalisms: Diasporas, Entanglements, Transruptions* (London: Zed Books).

Hallin, D. and Mancini, P. (2004) *Comparing Media Systems: Three Models of Media and Politics* (Cambridge: Cambridge University Press).

Hanitzsch, T. and Hanusch, F. (2012) 'Does Gender Determine Journalists' Professional Views? A Reassessment Based on Cross-National Evidence', *European Journal of Communication*, 27(3), 257–77.

Harcup, T. (2005) '"I'm Doing This to Change the World": Journalism in Alternative and Mainstream Media', *Journalism Studies*, 6(3), 361–74.

Harcup, T. (2011) 'Alternative Journalism as Active Citizenship', *Journalism*, 12(1), 15–31.

Hardin, M. and Whiteside, E. (2009) 'Token Responses to Gendered Newsrooms: Factors in the Career-Related Decisions of Female Newspaper Sports Journalists', *Journalism*, 10(5), 627–46.

Hargreaves, A. and Mahdjoub, D. (1997) 'Satellite Television Viewing among Ethnic Minorities in France', *European Journal of Communication*, 12(4), 459–477.

Harvey, S. (1998) 'Doing It My Way – Broadcasting Regulation in Capitalist Cultures: The Case of "Fairness" and "Impartiality"', *Media, Culture and Society*, 20(4), 535–556.

Heins, M. and Freedman, E. (2007) 'Foreword: Reclaiming the First Amendment: Constitutional Theories of Media Reform', *Hofstra Law Review*, 35(3), 917–36.

Herman, E.S. (1997) 'The Externalities Effects of Commercial and Public Broadcasting' in P. Golding and G. Murdock (eds) *The Political Economy of the Media Vol. 1* (Cheltenham: Edward Elgar Publishing Ltd.).

Herman, E. and McChesney, R. (1997) *The Global Media: The New Missionaries of Corporate Capitalism* (London: Cassell).

Hesmondhalgh, D. (2013) *The Cultural Industries*, 3rd edn (London: Sage).

Himelboim, Z., Chang, T. and McCreery, S. (2010) 'International Network of Foreign News Coverage: Old Global Hierarchies in a New Online World', *Journalism and Mass Communication Quarterly*, 87(2), 297–314.

Hopkins, P. (2012) 'Deconstructing *Good Times* and *The Cosby Show*: In Search of My "Authentic" Black Experience', *Journal of Black Studies*, 48(3), 954–75.

Horsti, K. and Hultén, G. (2011) 'Directing Diversity: Managing Cultural Diversity Media Policies in Finnish and Swedish Public Service Broadcasting', *Journal of Cultural Studies*, 14(2), 209–27.

Horsti, K., Hultén, G. and Titley, G. (2014) (eds) *National Conversations: Public Service Media and Cultural Diversity in Europe* (Bristol: Intellect).

Hospodárske noviny (2015) 'Sú Utečenci Hrozbou pre Slovensko? Pozrite Sa, Ako Sa Líšia Fico a Kiska' [Are Refugees a Threat to Slovakia? See how Different Fico and Kiska Are] http://hn.hnonline.sk/slovensko-119/su-utecenci-hrozbou-pre-slovensko-pozrite-sa-ako-sa-lisia-fico-a-kiska-903116, date accessed 16 February 2016.

Hourigan, N. (2001) 'New Social Movement Theory and Minority Language Television Campaigns', *European Journal of Communication*, 16(1), 77–100.

House of Commons Culture, Media and Sport Committee (2015) 'Privacy and Media Intrusion', http://www.parliament.the-stationeryoffice.co.uk/pa/cm200203/cmselect/cmcumeds/458/458.pdf, date accessed 30 October 2015.

House of Lords, Communications Committee (2012) Third Report: The Future of Investigative Journalism, http://www.publications.parliament.uk/pa/ld201012/ldselect/ldcomuni/256/25602.htm, date accessed 10 October 2015.

Hoyng, R. (2014) 'Circuits of Shock and Bunk: The Politics of the Dutch Blogosphere', *International Journal of Cultural Studies*, 17(4), 347–62.

Hozic, A. (2008) 'Democratizing Media, Welcoming Big Brother: Media in Bosnia and Herzegovina' in K. Jakubowicz and M. Sükösd (eds) *Finding the Right Place on the Map* (Bristol: Intellect).

Hultén, G. (2009) 'Diversity Disorders: Ethnicity and Newsroom Cultures', *Conflict and Communication Online* 8(2).

Humprecht, E. and Büchel, F. (2013) 'More of the Same or Marketplace of Opinions? Comparison of Diversity in Online News Reporting', *The International Journal of Press/Politics*, 18(4), 436–61.

Huq, R. (2003) 'From the Margins to the Mainstream? Representations of British Asian Youth Musical Cultural Expression from Bhangra to Asian Underground Music', *Young: Nordic Journal of Youth Research*, 11(1), 29–48.

Husband, C. (1998) 'Differentiated Citizenship and the Multi-Ethnic Public Sphere', *The Journal of International Communication*, 5(1&2), 134–48.

Husband, C. (2000) 'Media and the Public Sphere in Multi-Ethnic Societies' in S. Cottle (ed.) *Ethnic Minorities and the Media: Changing Cultural Boundaries* (Buckingham: Open University Press).

iab (2015) 'Audience Reach Measurement Guidelines', http://www.iab.com/wp-content/uploads/2015/06/AudienceReachMeasurementGuidelines.pdf, date accessed 30 October 2015.

Ingber, S. (1984) 'The Marketplace of Ideas', *Duke Law Journal*, 1984(1), 1–91.

Inniss, L. and Feagin, J. (1995) 'The Cosby Show: The View from The Black Middle Class', *Journal of Black Studies*, 25(6), 692–711.

International Commission for the Study of Communication Problems (undated) *The World of News Agencies* (Paris: UNESCO), http://unesdoc.unesco.org/images/0003/000370/037078eb.pdf, date accessed 20 October 2015.

International Commission for the Study of Communication Problems (1980) *Communication and Society Today and Tomorrow, Many Voices, One World: Towards a New More Just and More Efficient World Information and Communication Order* (Paris: UNESCO, London: Kogan Page and New York: Unipub), http://unesdoc.unesco.org/images/0004/000400/040066eb.pdf, date accessed 20 October 2015.

Jakubowicz, K. (1999) 'The Genie is Out of the Bottle', *Media Studies Journal*, 13(3), 52–9.

Journal of Ethnic and Migration Studies (2015) Special issue 'Migrants, Minorities, and the Media: Information, Representations, and Participation in the Public Sphere', 41(6).

Jufereva, M. and Lauk, E. (2015) 'Minority Language Media and Journalists in the Context of Societal Integration in Estonia', *Medijske Studije/Media Studies*, 6(11), 51–66.

Juluri, V. (2002) 'Music Television and the Invention of Youth Culture in India', *Television and New Media*, 3(4), 367–86.

Kahne, J., Middaugh, E., Lee, N. and Feezell, J. (2011) 'Youth Online Activity and Exposure to Diverse Perspectives', *New Media and Society*, 14(3), 492–512.

Kang, C. (2014) 'Netflix Has Hits, Emmys and Subscribers. But Can It Survive Its Fight with Cable?', https://www.washingtonpost.com/business/technology/netflix-has-hits-emmys-and-subscribers-but-can-it-survive-its-fight-with-cable/2014/07/10/73638bba-02c3-11e4-8572-4b1b969b6322_story.html, date accessed 20 October 2015.

Karppinen, K. (2007) 'Making a Difference to Media Pluralism: A Critique of the Pluralistic Consensus in European Media Policy' in B. Cammaerts and N. Carpentier (eds) *Reclaiming the Media: Communication Rights and Democratic Media Roles* (Bristol: Intellect).

Katz, R. (2012) *The Impact of Broadband on the Economy: Research to Date and Policy Issues* (Geneva: International Telecommunication Union), https://www.itu.int/ITU-D/treg/broadband/ITU-BB-Reports_Impact-of-Broadband-on-the-Economy.pdf, date accessed 19 February 2016.

Keane, J. (1991) *Media and Democracy* (Cambridge: Polity Press).

Kerner, O. (1968) *Report of the National Advisory Commission on Civil Disorders* (New York: Bantam).

Kleinsteuber, H. (2004) 'The Internet between Regulation and Governance' in *Self-Regulation, Co-regulation, State Regulation* (Vienna: Organization for Security and Cooperation in Europe), http://www.osce.org/fom/13844?download=true, date accessed 16 February 2016.

Klinenberg, E. (2008) *Fighting for Air: The Battle to Control America's Media* (New York: Henry Holt and Co).

Knight Foundation (2015) 'Gaining Ground: How Nonprofit News Ventures Seek Sustainability', http://knightfoundation.org/features/nonprofitnews-2015, date accessed 10 October 2015.

Kochhar, R. and Fry, R. (2014) 'Wealth Inequality has Widened along Racial, Ethnic Lines since End of Great Recession', Pew Research Center, http://www.pewresearch.org/fact-tank/2014/12/12/racial-wealth-gaps-great-recession/, date accessed 30 October 2015.

Konieczna, M. and Robinson, S. (2014) 'Emerging News Non-Profits: A Case Study for Rebuilding Community Trust?', *Journalism*, 15(8), 968–86.

Kosnick, K. (2000) 'Building Bridges: Media for Migrants and the Public-Service Mission in Germany', *European Journal of Cultural Studies*, 3(3), 319–42.

Krausova, A. and Vargas-Silva, C. (2013) 'London: Census Profile', http://www.migrationobservatory.ox.ac.uk/briefings/london-census-profile, date accessed 20 October 2015.

Kruglak, T. (1968) 'A Proposal: Apply Doctrine of Fairness to World News Coverage', *Journalism & Mass Communication Educator*, 23(3), 21–4.

Ksiazek, T., Peer, L. and Lessard, K. (2014) 'User Engagement with Online News: Conceptualizing Interactivity and Exploring the Relationship between Online News Videos and User Comments', *New Media and Society*, 1–19.

Kumar, P. (2011) 'Shrinking Foreign Coverage', *American Journalism Review*, December/January, http://ajrarchive.org/article.asp?id=4998, date accessed 20 October 2015.

Kundnani, A. (2015) *The Muslims are Coming! Islamophobia, Extremism and the Domestic War on Terrorism* (London: Verso).

Kymlicka, W. (1995) *Multicultural Citizenship: A Liberal Theory of Minority Rights* (Oxford: Clarendon Press).

Kymlicka, W. (2003) 'Canadian Multiculturalism in Historical and Comparative Perspective: Is Canada Unique?', *Forum Constitutionnel*, 13(1).

Kymlicka, W. (2012) *Multiculturalism: Success, Failure and the Future* (Washington DC: Migration Policy Institute), http://www.migrationpolicy.org/research/TCM-multiculturalism-success-failure, date accessed 20 October 2015.

Latzer, M. (2009) 'Information and Communication Technology Innovations: Radical and Disruptive?', *New Media and Society*, 11(4), 599–619.

Lavie, A. and Lehman-Wilzig, S. (2005) 'The Method is the Message: Explaining Inconsistent Findings in Gender and News Production Research', *Journalism: Theory, Practice and Criticism* 6(1), 66–89.

Learmonth, M. (2015) 'Can HBO Win the War Against Netflix?' Newsweek, http://www.newsweek.com/2015/03/20/can-hbo-win-war-against-netflix-312562.html, date accessed 20 October 2015.

Lears, J. (1994) *Fables of Abundance: A Cultural History of Advertising in America* (New York: Basic Books).

Lee, M. (2011) 'Google Ads and the Blindspot Debate', *Media Culture Society*, 33(3), 433–47.

Lentin, A. and Titley, G. (2011) 'The Crisis of "Multiculturalism" in Europe: Mediated Minarets, Intolerable Subjects', *European Journal of Cultural Studies*, 15(2), 123–38.

Lind, R.A. (2003) (ed.) *Race/Gender/Media: Considering Diversity across Audiences, Content and Producers* (Boston, MA: Allyne & Bacon).

Lorber, J. and Farrell, S. (1991) *The Social Construction of Gender* (London: Sage).

Loughborough University (2015) 'General Election 2015', http://blog.lboro. ac.uk/general-election/media-coverage-of-the-2015-campaign-report-5/, date accessed 30 October 2015.

Lunt, P. and Livingstone, S. (2012) *Media Regulation: Governance and the Interests of Citizens and Consumers* (London: Sage).

Lutz, A. (2012) 'These 6 Corporations Control 90% of the Media in America', *Business Insider,* http://www.businessinsider.com/these-6-corporations-control-90-of-the-media-in-america-2012-6?IR=T, date accessed 10 October 2015.

Machill, M. (1998) 'Euronews: The First European News Channel as a Case Study for Media Industry Development in Europe and for Spectra of Transnational Journalism Research', *Media, Culture and Society*, 20(3), 427–50.

Mackey, R. (2015) 'Hungarian Leader Rebuked for Saying Muslim Migrants Must Be Blocked "To Keep Europe Christian"', *The New York Times*, http://mobile.nytimes.com/2015/09/04/world/europe/hungarian-leader-rebuked-for-saying-muslim-migrants-must-be-blocked-to-keep-europe-christian.html?referer=&_r=0, date accessed 15 November 2015.

Madianou, M. and Miller, D. (2011) *Migration and New Media: Transnational Families and Polymedia* (New York: Routledge).

Majone, G. (1994) 'Paradoxes of Privatization and Deregulation', *Journal of European Public Policy*, 1(1), 53–69.

Malik, S. (2012) 'The Indian Family on UK Reality Television: Convivial Culture in Salient Contexts', *Television and New Media*, 14(6), 510–528.

Malik, S. (2013) '"Creative Diversity": UK Public Service Broadcasting After Multiculturalism', *Popular Communication: The International Journal of Media and Culture*, 11(3), 227–41.

Mansell, R. (2004) 'Political Economy, Power and New Media', *New Media Society*, 6(1), 74–83.

Mansell, R. and Raboy, M. (2011) *The Handbook of Global Media and Communication Policy* (Hoboken, NJ: Wiley-Blackwell).

Mapp, T. (1979) 'Beyond Numbers: The Role of the Black Journalist in the News Media', *Journal of Communication Inquiry*, 5(1), 3–19.

Maras, S. (2012) *Objectivity in Journalism* (Cambridge: Polity).

Marshall, T.H. (1950) *Citizenship and Social Class and Other Essays* (Cambridge University Press).

Martin, P. (2003) '"Said and Done" Versus "Saying and Doing": Gendering Practices, Practicing Gender at Work', *Gender & Society*, 17(3), 342–66.

Mason, R. (2015) 'Nigel Farage Opposes EU action to Tackle Migrant Deaths in Mediterranean', *The Guardian*, http://www.theguardian.com/politics/ 2015/apr/20/nigel-farage-opposes-eu-action-to-tackle-migrant-deaths-in-mediterranean, date accessed 15 November 2015.

Mattelart, T. and Hargreaves, A. (2014) '"Diversity" Policies, Integration and Internal Security: The Case of France', *Global Media and Communication*, 10(3), 275–287.

Mayor of London (2015) '20 Facts about London's Culture' https://www.london. gov.uk/what-we-do/arts-and-culture/vision-and-strategy/20-facts-about-london%E2%80%99s-culture, date accessed 15 November 2015.

McCann, K. (2013) 'The Diversity Policy Model and Assessment of the Policy: Debates and Challenges of (Media) Diversity', *Sage Open*, 1–12.

McChesney, R.W. (2003) 'Theses on Media Deregulation', *Media, Culture and Society*, 25(1), 125–33.

McChesney, R. (2004) *The Problem of the Media: U.S. Communications Politics in the 21st Century* (New York: Monthly Review Press).

McCluskey, M. and Hmielowski, J. (2011) 'Opinion Expression during Social Conflict: Comparing Online Reader Comments and Letters to the Editor', *Journalism*, 13(3), 303–19.

McGonagle, T. (2008–9) 'European Parliament: Resolution on Community Media in Europe', *IRIS: Legal Observations of the European Audiovisual Observatory*, no.104, http://merlin.obs.coe.int/iris/2008/9/article104.en.html, date accessed 10 October 2015.

McKenna, A. (2000) 'Emerging Issues Surrounding the Convergence of the Telecommunications, Broadcasting and Information Technology Sectors', *Information and Communications Technology Law*, 9(2), 93–128.

McLuhan, M. (1962) *The Gutenberg Galaxy: The Making of Typographic Man* (Toronto: University of Toronto Press).

McManus, J.H. (1992) 'What Kind of Commodity Is News?', *Communication Research*, 19(6), 787–805.

McNicholas, A. (2004) 'Wrenching the Machine Around: *EastEnders*, the BBC and Institutional Change', *Media, Culture & Society*, 26(4), 491–512.

McQuail, D. (1992) 'The Netherlands: Safeguarding Freedom and Diversity Under Multichannel Conditions' in J.G. Blumler (ed.) *Television and the Public Interest* (London: Sage).

McQuail, D. (1992a) *Media Performance: Mass Communication and the Public Interest* (London: Sage).

Media Insight Project (2015) How Millennials Get News: Inside the Habits of America's First Digital Generation, http://www.americanpressinstitute .org/publications/reports/survey-research/millennials-news/, date accessed 10 October 2015.

Meier, J. and Trappel, W.A. (1998) 'Media Concentration and the Public Interest' in D. McQuail and K. Siune (eds) *Media Policy; Convergence, Concentration and Commerce* (London: Sage).

Metykova, M. (2005) *Regulating Public Service Broadcasting: The Cases of the Czech Republic, Slovakia and Ireland*, PhD dissertation (Brno: Masaryk University).

Metykova, M. and Preston, P. (2009) 'An Elusive "European" Public Sphere?: The Role of Shared Journalistic Cultures' in A. Charles (ed.) *Media in the Enlarged Europe: Politics, Policy and Industry* (Bristol: Intellect).

Metykova, M. (2010) 'Only a Mouse Click Away from Home: Transnational Practices of Eastern European Migrants in the United Kingdom', *Social Identities; Journal for the Study of Race, Nation and Culture*, 16(3), 325–38.

Metykova, M. (2013) 'Media and Advertising – the Interests of Citizens and Consumers' in C. Wharton (ed.) *Advertising as Culture* (Bristol: Intellect).

Metykova, M. (2015) 'European Media Policy: Why Margins Actually Matter' in E. Thorsen, D. Jackson, H. Savigny and J. Alexander (eds) *Media, Margins and Civic Agency* (Basingstoke: Palgrave Macmillan).

Mihelj, S. (2011) *Media Nations: Communicating Belonging and Exclusion in the Modern World* (London and New York: Palgrave Macmillan).

Miller, T. (2007) *Cultural Citizenship: Cosmopolitanism, Consumerism, and Television in a Neoliberal Age* (Philadelphia: Temple University).

Mills, E. (2014) 'Why Do the Best Jobs Go to Men?', *British Journalism Review*, 25(3), 17–23.

Mitchell, A. and Matsa, K.E. (2015) 'The Declining Value of U.S. Newspapers', Pew Research Center, http://www.pewresearch.org/fact-tank/2015/05/22/the-declining-value-of-u-s-newspapers/, date accessed 30 October 2015.

Mitchell, A., Holcomb, J. and Page, D. (2015) 'Local News in a Digital Age', Pew Research Center, http://www.journalism.org/2015/03/05/local-news-in-a-digital-age/, date accessed 10 October 2015.

Modood, T. and Ahmad, F. (2007) 'British Muslim Perspectives on Multiculturalism', *Theory, Culture and Society*, 24(2), 187–213.

Mohammadi, A. (1997) (ed.) *International Communication and Globalization* (London: Sage).

Molnar, P. (1999) 'Transforming Hungarian Broadcasting', *Media Studies Journal*, 13(3), 90–7.

Moores, S. (1993) *Interpreting Audiences: The Ethnography of Media Consumption* (London: Sage).

Moores, S. and Metykova, M. (2010) '"I Didn't Realize How Attached I Am": On the Environmental Experiences of Trans-European Migrants', *European Journal of Cultural Studies*, 13(2), 171–89.

Morley, D. (1992) *Television, Audiences and Cultural Studies* (London: Routledge).

Morley, D. and Robins, K. (1995) *Spaces of Identity: Global Media, Electronic Landscapes and Cultural Boundaries* (London: Routledge).

Murdock, G. (1990) 'Redrawing the Map of the Communications Industries: Concentration and Ownership in the Era of Privatization' in M. Ferguson (ed.) *Public Communication – The New Imperatives: Future Directions for Media Research* (London: Sage).

Murdock, G. (1992) 'Citizens, Consumers, and Public Culture' in M. Skovmand and K.C. Schrøder (eds) *Media Cultures: Reappraising Transnational Media* (London: Routledge).

Murdock, G. (1997) 'Redrawing the Map of the Communications Industries: Concentration and Ownership in the Era of Privatization' in P. Golding and G. Murdock (eds) *The Political Economy of the Media* (Cheltenham: Edward Elgar).

Murdock, G. (2004) 'Building the Digital Commons: Public Broadcasting in the Age of the Internet. The 2004 Spry Memorial Lecture', https://pantherfile.uwm.edu/type/www/116/Theory_OtherTexts/Theory/Murdock_BuildingDigitalCommons.pdf , date accessed 20 October 2015.

Myllylahti, M. (2014) 'Newspaper Paywalls – the Hype and the Reality', *Digital Journalism*, 2(2), 179–194.

NABJ (2015) NABJ Releases 2012 Television Newsroom Management and Network Diversity Census, http://www.nabj.org/news/103235/NABJ-Releases-2012-Television-Newsroom-Management-and-Network-Diversity-Census.htm, date accessed 20 October 2015.

Negt, O. and Kluge, A. (1993) *Public Sphere and Experience: Toward an Analysis of the Bourgeois and Proletarian Public Sphere* (Minneapolis: University of Minnesota Press).

New York Times, The (2014) 'Innovation', https://www.scribd.com/doc/224332847/NYT-Innovation-Report-2014#download, date accessed 30 October 2015.

Nielsen (2014) 'The Bilingual Brain', http://www.nielsen.com/us/en/insights/reports/2014/the-bilingual-brain.html, date accessed 30 October 2015.

Nielsen (2015) 'A Timeline of Important Nielsen People Meter Moments', http://www.nielsen.com/content/dam/corporate/us/en/newswire/uploads/2012/08/Nielsen-People-Meter-Timeline.png, date accessed 20 October 2015.

No author (2005) Special issue 'The MacBride Report – 25 Years Later', *Javnost – The Public*, 12(3).

North, L. (2014) 'Still a "Blokes' Club": The Motherhood Dilemma in Journalism', *Journalism*, 1–17.

Nussbaum, E. (7 July 2014) 'Lockdown: The Lessons of "Orange is the New Black" and "Louie"', *The New Yorker*, http://www.newyorker.com/magazine/2014/07/07/lockdown-2, date accessed 19 February 2016.

O'Connor, A. (2006) *Raymond Williams* (Lanham: Rowman & Littlefield).

Ofcom (2014) 'The Communications Market: Digital Radio Report. Ofcom's Fifth Annual Digital Progress Report', http://stakeholders.ofcom.org.uk/market-data-research/other/radio-research/digital-radio-reports/digital-radio-2014/, date accessed 10 October 2015.

Ofcom (2015) 'CMR 2015 Annex Changes in TV Viewing Habits', http://stakeholders.ofcom.org.uk/binaries/research/cmr/cmr15/CMR_2015_Annex_Changes_in_TV_viewing_habits.pdf, date accessed 20 October 2015.

Ofcom (2015a) 'Broadcasting Code', http://stakeholders.ofcom.org.uk/broad-casting/broadcast-codes/broadcast-code/impartiality/, date accessed 30 October 2015.

Ofcom (2015b) 'Ofcom Rules on Party Political and Referendum Broadcasts', http://stakeholders.ofcom.org.uk/broadcasting/guidance/programme-guidance/ppbrules/, date accessed 30 October 2015.

Ofcom (2015c) 'Ofcom Statement on Party Election Broadcasts' http://media.ofcom.org.uk/news/2015/major-parties-statement/, date accessed 30 October 2015.

ONS (2015) 2011 Census: Key Statistics for England and Wales, March 2011, http://www.ons.gov.uk/ons/rel/census/2011-census/key-statistics-for-local-authorities-in-england-and-wales/stb-2011-census-key-statistics-for-england-and-wales.html#tab---Ethnic-group, date accessed 20 October 2015.

Otto, F. and Meyer, C. (2012) 'Missing the Story? Changes in Foreign News Reporting and Their Implications for Conflict Prevention', *Media, War and Conflict*, 5(3), 205–21.

Ozohu-Suleiman, Y. (2014) 'War Journalism on Israel/ Palestine: Does Contra-Flow Really Make a Difference?', *Media, War & Conflict*, 7(1), 85–103.

Painter, J. (2008) *Counter-Hegemonic News: A Case Study of Al-Jazeera English and Telesur* (Oxford: Reuters Institute for the Study of Journalism).

Pariser, E. (2011) *The Filter Bubble: What the Internet is Hiding from You* (London: Penguin Books).

PCMLP (2004) *Self-Regulation of Digital Media Converging on the Internet: Industry Codes of Conduct in Sectoral Analysis* (Oxford: Oxford University Programme in Comparative Media Law and Policy), http://pcmlp.socleg.ox.ac.uk/research/archived-projects/, date accessed 19 February 2016.

Perlman, A. (2012) 'Whitewashing Diversity: The Conservative Attack on the "Stealth Fairness Doctrine"', *Television & New Media*, 13(4), 353–73.

Peters, C. and Broersma, M. (2013) (eds) *Rethinking Journalism: Trust and Participation in a Transformed Media Landscape* (London: Routledge).

Petley, J. (2012) 'The Leveson Inquiry: Journalism Ethics and Press Freedom', *Journalism*, 13(4), 529–38.

Pew Research Center (2015) *Multiracial in America: Proud, Diverse and Growing in Numbers* (Washington, DC: Pew Research Center: Social and Demographic Trends), http://www.pewsocialtrends.org/files/2015/06/2015-06-11_multiracial-in-america_final-updated.pdf, date accessed 10 October 2015.

Philip, G. and Tsoi, S.H. (1988) 'Regulation and Deregulation of Telecommunications: The Economic and Political Realities. Part I: The United States.' *Journal of Information Science*, 14, 257–64.

Picard, R. (1989) *Media Economics: Concepts and Issues* (London: Sage).

Picard, R. and Chon, B.S. (2004) 'Managing Competition through Barriers to Entry and Channel Availability in the Changing Regulatory Environment', *JMM – International Journal on Media Management*, 6(3&4), 168–75.

Picard, R. (2005) 'Unique Characteristics and Business Dynamics of Media Products', *Journal of Media Business Studies*, 2(2), 61–9.

Pitcher, B. (2009) *The Politics of Multiculturalism: Race and Racism in Contemporary Britain* (Basingstoke: Palgrave Macmillan).

Polonska-Kimunguyi, E. and Kimunguyi, P. (2011) 'The Making of the Europeans: Media in the Construction of Pan-National Identity', *The International Communication Gazette*, 73(6), 507–23.

Poole, E. (2002) *Reporting Islam: Media Representations of British Muslims* (London: I.B.Tauris).

Prague Post (2013) 'Monday News Briefing – Nov. 4, 2013', http://www.prague-post.com/czech-news/27369-monday-news-briefing-nov-4, date accessed 30 October 2015.

Pritchard, D. and Stonbely, S. (2007) 'Racial Profiling in the Newsroom', *J&MC Quarterly*, 84(2), 231–48.

Raboy, M. (1996) (ed.) *Public Broadcasting for the 21st Century* (Luton: University of Luton Press).

Raeijmaekers, D. and Maeseele, P. (2015) 'Media, Pluralism and Democracy: What's in a Name?', *Media, Culture and Society*, 37(7), 1042–59.

Redden, J. and Witschge, T. (2009) 'A New News Order? Online News Content Examined' in N. Fenton (ed.) *New Media, Old News: Journalism and Democracy in the Digital Age* (London: Routledge).

Reese, S., Gandy, O. and Grant, A. (2001) (eds) *Framing Public Life: Perspectives on Media and Our Understanding of the Social World* (Abingdon: Taylor and Francis).

Reid, A. (2015) 'Women Outnumber Men on UK Journalism Degrees', https://www.journalism.co.uk/news/women-outnumber-men-on-uk-journalism-degrees/s2/a563890/, date accessed 20 October 2015.

Rieder, B. and Sire, G. (2014) 'Conflicts of Interest and Incentives to Bias: A Microeconomic Critique of Google's Tangled Position on the Web', *New Media and Society*, 16(2), 195–211.

Rienzo, C. and Vargas-Silva, C. (2015) *Briefing: Migrants in the UK: An Overview*, 5th revision (University of Oxford: The Migration Observatory), http://www.migrationobservatory.ox.ac.uk/briefings/migrants-uk-overview.

Robbins, B. (1993) (ed.) *The Phantom Public Sphere* (Minneapolis: University of Minnesota Press).

Robertson, A. (2014) 'Atlas Reports: Global Television Constructions of Economic Crisis', *European Journal of Communication*, 29(5), 618–25.

Robertson, R. (1990) 'Mapping the Global Condition: Globalization as the Central Concept' in M. Featherstone (ed.) *Global Culture* (London: Sage).

Robins, K. (2001) 'Becoming Anybody: Thinking against the Nation and through the City', *City*, 5(1), 77–90.

Robins, K. (2007) 'Transnational Cultural Policy and European Cosmopolitanism', *Cultural Politics*, 3(2), 147–74.

Rovio (2014) 'Rovio Entertainment Reports 2013 Financial Results', http://www.rovio.com/rovio-entertainment-reports-2013-financial-results, date accessed 26 January 2016.

RTDNA (2015) Women and Minorities in Newsrooms, http://www.rtdna. org/article/women_minorities_make_newsroom_gains#.VW1q2c9Viko, date accessed 20 October 2015.

Rush, R.R., Oukrup, C.J. and Creedon, P.J. (2004) *Seeking Equity for Women in Journalism and Mass Communication Education: A 30-Year Update* (Mahwah, NJ: Lawrence Erlbaum Associates).

Saha, A. (2012) '"Beards, Scarves, Halal Meat, Terrorists, Forced Marriage": Television Industries and the Production of "Race"', *Media Culture and Society*, 34(4), 424–38.

Samuel-Azran, T. (2013) 'Al-Jazeera, Qatar, and New Tactics in State-Sponsored Media Diplomacy', *American Behavioural Scientist*, 57(9), 1293–311.

Sarikakis, K. (2007) *Media and Cultural Policy in the European Union* (Amsterdam: Rodopi).

Save the Internet (2015) 'How to Save the Internet', http://www.savetheinternet .com/sti-home, date accessed 20 February 2016.

Schiller, H.I. (1969) *Mass Communication and American Empire* (Boston, MA: Beacon Press).

Schoch, L. (2013) '"Feminine" Writing: The Effect of Gender on the Work of Women Sports Journalists in the Swiss Daily Press', *Media, Culture & Society*, 35(6), 708–23.

Scholten, P. and Verbeek, S. (2015) 'Politicization and Expertise: Changing Research–Policy Dialogues on Migrant Integration in Europe', *Science and Public Policy*, 42(2), 188–200.

Schudson, M. (1995) *The Power of News* (Cambridge, MA and London: Harvard University Press).

Schudson, M. (2001) 'The Objectivity Norm in American Journalism', *Journalism*, 2(2), 149–70.

Schudson, M. (2003) *The Sociology of News* (New York and London: W.W. Norton).

Seaton, J. (2015) *Pinkoes and Traitors: The BBC and the Nation, 1974–1987* (London: Profile Books).

Segev, E. (2015) 'Visible and Invisible Countries: News Flow Theory Revised', *Journalism*, 15(3), 412–28.

Shoemaker, P.J., Eichholz, M., Kim, E. and Wrigley, B. (2001) 'Individual and Routine Forces in Gatekeeping', *Journalism and Mass Communication Quarterly*, 78(2), 233–46.

Shoemaker, P. and Vos, T. (2009) *Gatekeeping Theory* (Abingdon: Taylor and Francis).

Siefert, M. (2007) 'Twentieth-century Culture, "Americanization" and European Audiovisual Space' in K. Jarausch and T. Lindenberger (eds) *Conflicted Memories: Europeanizing Contemporary Histories* (New York: Berghahn Books).

Silverstone, R. (2005) (ed.) *Media, Technology and Everyday Life in Europe: From Information to Communication* (Aldershot: Ashgate).

Simons, N. (2013) 'BBC Presenters Have "Deeply Held Left-Wing Political Views", Complain Tory MPs', *The Huffington Post UK*, http://www .huffingtonpost.co.uk/2013/10/22/bbc-conservative-bias_n_4141058.html, date accessed 10 October 2015.

Sinclair, J. (2009) 'Minorities, Media, Marketing and Marginalization', *Global Media and Communication*, 5(2), 177–196.

Singer, J. (2014) 'User-Generated Visibility: Secondary Gatekeeping in a Shared Media Space', *New Media & Society*, 16(1), 55–73.

Siune, K. and Hultén, O. (1998) 'Does Public Broadcasting Have a Future?' in D. McQuail and K. Siune (eds) *Media Policy: Convergence, Concentration and Commerce* (London: Sage).

Sivanandan, A. (2006) 'Britain's Shame: From Multiculturalism to Nativism' (London: Institute of Race Relations), http://www.irr.org.uk/news/britains-shame-from-multiculturalism-to-nativism/, date accessed 10 October 2015.

Skjerdal, T.S. (2011) 'Journalists or Activists? Self-Identity in the Ethiopian Diaspora Online Community', *Journalism*, 12(6), 727–44.

Sledge, M. (2014) 'Chuck Schumer Wants FCC to Reclassify Broadband Providers for Net Neutrality', http://www.huffingtonpost.com/2014/07/11/chuck-schumer-net-neutrality_n_5579131.html, date accessed 20 November 2015.

Smith, G.R. (2010) 'Politicians and the News Media: How Elite Attacks Influence Perceptions of Media Bias', *International Journal of Press/Politics*, 15(3) 319–343.

Somaiya, R. (2014) 'The Times Co. Reports a 2.6% Rise in Revenue', *The New York Times*, http://www.nytimes.com/2014/04/25/business/media/times-co-reports-increased-advertising-and-circulation-revenue.html?_r=0, date accessed 30 October 2015.

Sparks, C. with Reading, A. (1998) *Communism, Capitalism and the Mass Media* (London: Sage).

Squires, K. (2014) *The Post-Racial Mystique: Media and Race in the Twenty-First Century* (New York: New York University Press).

Stanford University (2015) 'Immigration and Integration Policy Lab', http://immigrationlab.stanford.edu/, date accessed 30 October 2015.

Sullivan, M. (2015) 'A "Darker Narrative" of Print's Future From Clay Shirky', *The New York Times*, http://publiceditor.blogs.nytimes.com/2015/04/10/a-darker-narrative-of-prints-future-from-clay-shirky/?_r=0, date accessed 30 October 2015.

Sunstein, C. (2009) *Republic.com 2.0.* (Princeton, NJ: Princeton University Press).

Swaine, J., Laughland, O. and Lartey, J. (2015) 'Black Americans Kiled by Police Twice as Likely to be Unarmed as White People', http://www.theguardian.com/us-news/2015/jun/01/black-americans-killed-by-police-analysis, date accessed 15 November 2015.

Swegman Brundage, G. (1972) 'Rationale for the Application of the Fairness Doctrine in Broadcast News', *Journalism & Mass Communication Quarterly*, 49(3), 531–37.

Sweney, M. (2014) 'London Live to Halt Entertainment Commissioning', *The Guardian*, http://www.theguardian.com/media/2014/aug/18/london-live-evgeny-lebedev-evening-standard, date accessed 30 October 2015.

Tandoc, E. (2014) 'Journalism is Twerking? How Web Analytics is Changing the Process of Gatekeeping', *New Media & Society*, 16(4), 559–75.

Tazanu, P.M. (2015) 'On the Liveness of Mobile Phone Mediation: Youth Expectations of Remittances and Narratives of Discontent in the Cameroonian Transnational Family', *Mobile Media and Communication*, 3(1), 20–35.

Terry, W. (2007) *Missing Pages: Black Journalists of Modern America: An Oral History* (New York: Basic Books).

Thussu, D.K. (2000) *International Communication – Continuity and Change* (London: Arnold).

Thussu, D. K. (2007) (ed.) Media on the Move: Global Flow and Contra-Flow (London: Routledge).

Tierney, S. (2007) (ed.) *Multiculturalism and the Canadian Constitution* (Vancouver and Toronto: UBCPress).

Titley, G. (2014) 'After the End of Multiculturalism: Public Service Media and Integrationist Imaginaries for the Governance of Difference', *Global Media and Communication*, 10(3), 247–60.

Travis, A. (2015) 'Theresa May's Plan To Censor TV Shows Condemned by Tory Cabinet Colleague', *The Guardian*, http://www.theguardian.com/world/2015/may/21/mays-plan-to-censor-tv-programmes-condemned-by-tory-cabinet-colleague, date accessed 30 October 2015.

Tremlett, A. (2014) 'Making a Difference without Creating a Difference: Super-Diversity as a New Direction for Research on Roma Minorities', *Ethnicities*, 14(6), 830–48.

Trilling, D. and Schoenbach, K. (2012) 'Skipping Current Affairs: The Non-Users of Online and Offline News', *European Journal of Communication*, 28(1), 35–51.

UNESCO (1953) *News Agencies: Their Structure and Operation* (Paris: UNESCO), http://unesdoc.unesco.org/images/0007/000734/073446eo.pdf, date accessed 10 October 2015.

UNESCO and UNDP (2013) *Creative Economy Report. Special Edition. Widening Local Development Pathways* (Paris: UNDP), http://www.unesco.org/culture/pdf/creative-economy-report-2013.pdf, date accessed 15 October 2015.

van Cuilenburg, J. and McQuail, D. (2003) 'Media Policy Paradigm Shifts Towards a New Communications Policy Paradigm', *European Journal of Communication*, 18(2), 181–207.

van den Bulck, H. (2001) 'Public Service Broadcasting and National Identity as a Project of Modernity', *Media, Culture and Society*, 23(1), 53–69.

van Deursen, A. and van Dijk, J. (2014) 'The Digital Divide Shifts to Differences in Usage', *New Media & Society*, 16(3), 507–26.

van Zoonen, L. (1998) 'One of the Girls? The Changing Gender of Journalism' in C. Carter, G. Branston and S. Allan (eds) *News, Gender and Power* (London: Routledge).

Vancea, M. and Olivera, N. (2013) 'E-migrant Women in Catalonia: Mobile Phone Use and Maintenance of Family Relationships', *Gender, Technology and Development*, 17(2), 179–203.

Varis, T. (1986) 'Trends in International Television Flow', *International Political Science Review*, 7(3), 235–249.

Vertovec, S. (1996) 'Berlin Multikulti: Germany, "Foreigners" and "World Openness"', *New Community*, 22(3), 381–99.

Vertovec, S. (1999) 'Conceiving and Researching Transnationalism', *Ethnic and Racial Studies*, 22(2), 447–62.

Vertovec, S. (2007) 'Super-Diversity and its Implications', *Ethnic and Racial Studies*, 30(6), 1024–54.

Vos, T.P. and Li, Y. (2013) 'Justifying Commercialization: Legitimating Discourses and the Rise of American Advertising', *Journalism & Mass Communication Quarterly*, 90(3), 559–80.

Wallis, C. (2013) *Technomobility in China: Young Migrant Women and Mobile Phones* (New York and London: New York University Press).

Waltz, M. (2005) *Alternative and Activist Media* (Edinburgh: Edinburgh University Press).

Warrick, J. (2011) 'Clinton: U.S. Losing Global Public-Relations Battle to "Baywatch" and Wrestling', *The Washington Post*, http://www.washingtonpost.com/wp-dyn/content/article/2011/03/02/AR2011030206898.html, date accessed 10 October 2015.

Watanabe, K. (2013) 'The Western Perspective in Yahoo! News and Google News: Quantitative Analysis of Geographic Coverage of Online News', *International Communication Gazette*, 75(2), 141–56.

Watts, M.D., Domke, D., Shah, D.V. and Fan, D.P. (1999) 'Elite Cues and Media Bias in Presidential Elections: Explaining Public Perceptions of a Liberal Press', *Communication Research*, 26(2), 144–75.

Weaver, D. and Wilhoit, G.C. (1996) *The American Journalist in the 1990s* (Mahwah, NJ: Lawrence Erlbaum Associates).

Wharton, C. (2013) (ed.) *Advertising as Culture* (Bristol: Intellect).

White, D. Manning (1950) 'The "Gate Keeper": A Case Study in the Selection of News', *Journalism Quarterly*, 27(3), 383–90.

White House, The (2015) 'Remarks by the President in Eulogy for the Honorable Reverend Clementa Pinckney', https://www.whitehouse.gov/the-press-office/2015/06/26/remarks-president-eulogy-honorable-reverend-clementa-pinckney, date accessed 10 October 2015.

Williams, A., Barnett, S., Harte, D. and Townend, J. (2014) *The State of Hyperlocal Community News in the UK: Findings from a Survey of Practitioners* (Cardiff University, Birmingham City University and University of Westminster), https://hyperlocalsurvey.wordpress.com/, date accessed 12 October 2015.

Williams, H. (2014) 'Changing the National Narrative: Evolution in Citizenship and Integration in Germany, 2000–10', *Journal of Contemporary History*, 49(1), 54–74.

Williams, R. (1974) *Television: Technology and Cultural Form* (London: Fontana).

Willnat, L. and Weaver, D.H. (2014) *The American Journalist in the Digital Age: Key Findings* (Bloomington, IN: School of Journalism, Indiana University), http://news.indiana.edu/releases/iu/2014/05/2013-american-journalist-key-findings.pdf, date accessed 12 October 2015.

Wilson, C.C. (1991) *Black Journalists in Paradox: Historical Perspectives and Current Dilemmas* (New York, London: Greenwood).

Wilson, C.C. (2000) 'The Paradox and African American Journalists' in S. Cottle (ed.) *Ethnic Minorities and the Media* (Milton Keynes: Open University Press).

Wimmer, A. and Glick Schiller, N. (2002) 'Methodological Nationalism and Beyond: Nation-State Building, Migration and the Social Sciences', *Global Networks*, 2(4), 301–34.

Wimmer, A. (2007) 'How (Not) to Think about Ethnicity in Immigrant Societies: A Boundary Making Perspective', ESRC Centre on Migration, Policy and Society Working Paper No. 44, https://www.compas.ox.ac.uk/media/WP-2007-044-Wimmer_Ethnicity_Immigrant_Socities.pdf, date accessed 12 October 2015.

Winseck, D. (2002) 'Netscapes of Power: Convergence, Consolidation and Power in the Canadian Mediascape', *Media, Culture and Society*, 24(6), 795–819.

Winseck, D. and Pike, R.M. (2009) 'The Global Media and The Empire of Liberal Internationalism, Circa 1910–30', *Media History*, 15(1), 31–54.

Wojcieszak, M. (2007) 'Al Jazeera: A Challenge to Traditional Framing Research', *The International Communication Gazette*, 69(2), 115–28.

Wolseley, R.E. (1990) *The Black Press, U.S.A.*, 2nd edn (Ames, Iowa: Iowa State University Press).

Wood, L. (2014) 'Frozen: Parental Panic as Unexpected Disney Hit Leads to Merchandise Sellout', *The Guardian* http://www.theguardian.com/film/2014/may/17/frozen-film-disney-success-merchandise-sellout, date accessed 10 October 2015.

Worley, C. (2005) '"It's Not About Race. It's About The Community": New Labour and "Community Cohesion"', *Critical Social Policy*, 25(4), 483–96.

Ziegele, M. and Quiring, O. (2013) 'Conceptualizing Online Discussion Value. A Multidimensional Framework for Analyzing User Comments on Mass-Media Websites' in E.L. Cohen (ed.) *Communication Yearbook 37* (New York: Routledge).

Zoch, L.M. and VanSlyke Turk, J. (1998) 'Women Making News: Gender as a Variable in Source Selection and Use', *Journalism and Mass Communication Quarterly*, 75(4), 762–75.

Index

www.ingramcontent.com/pod-product-compliance
Lightning Source LLC
Chambersburg PA
CBHW050655280326
41932CB00015B/2924